JOHN PAUL II

THE ROAD TO BEATIFICATION

by
Jim Gallagher

*All booklets are published thanks to the
generous support of the members of the
Catholic Truth Society*

CATHOLIC TRUTH SOCIETY
PUBLISHERS TO THE HOLY SEE

Prayer for the intercession of Pope John Paul II

Blessed Trinity, We thank you
for having graced the Church
with Pope John Paul II
and for allowing the tenderness
of your Fatherly care,
the glory of the cross of Christ,
and the splendor of the Holy Spirit,
to shine through him.

Trusting fully in Your infinite mercy
and in the maternal intercession of Mary,
he has given us a living image of Jesus
the Good Shepherd, and has shown us
that holiness is the necessary measure
of ordinary Christian life
and is the way of achieving eternal
communion with you.

Grant us, by his intercession, and according to
Your will, the graces we implore, hoping that
he will soon be numbered among your saints.

Amen

❧ INTRODUCTION ❧

S ister Marie Simon-Pierre, of the French community of Little Sisters of Catholic Motherhood, was diagnosed in 2001 as having Parkinson's disease, the same illness as Pope John Paul II suffered in his later years. The disease is progressive and Sister Marie Simon-Pierre admitted that she was afraid of just how much her condition would deteriorate. So afraid, in fact, that she could not even bear to watch her beloved Pope on television. His condition was a reminder of how she would soon be.

Sister enjoyed her work on a maternity ward in Aix-en-Provence and was responsible for a number of staff. She remembered clearly the morning of 2nd June 2005. Speaking to journalists five and a half years later she recalled, "I was totally disabled and could no longer carry on."

She could no longer write legibly. She couldn't drive or move around easily and was in so much pain that she couldn't sleep. She had reached her limit and that morning she asked her Superior if she might resign her post and give up work. Her request to stand down was gently declined.

"Write John Paul II's name"

Instead, her Superior suggested that she ask the recently-deceased John Paul II to intercede for a cure for her. At that

Sister Marie Simon-Pierre

moment the two nuns experienced the atmosphere in the office change. "There came a great feeling of peace and serenity. I felt at peace and so did my Superior," recalled Sister. "This feeling of deep peace within and around us lasted for several minutes."

The Superior then asked her to write John Paul II's name on a piece of paper. The Parkinson's disease, though, had progressed so much that her left arm and hand trembled uncontrollably and she could not write. "Try with your right hand," said the Superior. Sister Marie told her she couldn't as that hand was shaking so much too. However, the Superior insisted she try. "You can do it", she said, "You can do it," Sister Marie later remembered. So she did her best to write John Paul's name on the paper. But it was illegible, really more like a scribble.

"Perhaps a miracle will happen if I just believe," Sister told herself. She returned to work and the normal life of the community. That night she slept well, not experiencing the usual insomnia caused by pain from the disease.

An interior joy

At 4.30 on the morning of the 3rd June she woke up feeling completely different. "I was no longer the same. I had an interior joy and great peace. Later on I was surprised by the movements I was able to make with my body," she reported.

At the same time, she experienced "a great urge to pray. It was not a set prayer-time but I prayed anyway." She reports that she went to the maternity ward chapel and there, before the tabernacle, prayed "with deep joy".

She joined the rest of the community for their usual 6am Mass. "I realised that my left arm was no longer immobile when I walked, but swung back and forth normally. During the Mass I became convinced that I was cured," said Sister Marie who comes from northern France. "I went to another sister and showed her my hand. It wasn't shaking. I said, 'John Paul has obtained my cure'. She looked at me wide-eyed and we stood in silence."

That day Sister Marie Simon-Pierre was able to work on the maternity ward, assisting at a caesarean section and registering the baby's birth in her own handwriting. She stopped taking her daily medication. Five days later her neurologist was stunned at her agility as she strolled into his office. He asked her if she had doubled her medication!

The Little Sister of Catholic Motherhood recounted all these events to journalists on 14th January 2011. On that very day Pope Benedict XVI approved her cure as the necessary miracle for the beatification of Pope John Paul II. The Vatican announced that the said beatification would take place in Rome on Divine Mercy Sunday, falling that year on 1st May. It would be the first time in over a thousand years that a pope had beatified his immediate predecessor. The speed of John Paul arriving at beatification following death would rival that of his great friend Mother Teresa!

Following Pope Benedict's announcement, the Vatican workforce had to go into overdrive to prepare for the expected huge crowds for the 1st May Beatification. There would be large television screens not only around St Peter's Square but down the Via della Conciliazione as well. No longer to be buried in the crypt of St Peter's, a new resting place was to be prepared for the new *beatus*. A tomb was prepared in the second side-chapel from the entrance to St Peter's (next to that housing the Pieta) and just before the Blessed Sacrament chapel wherein John Paul inaugurated daily exposition and adoration of the Blessed Sacrament during his pontificate. This was to cope with the expected crowds who would want to visit and pray at his tomb, which would be simply marked Beatus Ioannes Paulus.

When John Paul II's mortal remains were laid to rest on 8th April 2005, the media were calling it "the largest funeral the world has ever seen". Twenty-six years earlier, few had heard of the Polish cardinal who stepped onto the balcony of St Peter's Basilica after his election to the Chair of St Peter in October 1978.

A man from 'a far country'

His first words were of reassurance. "Don't be afraid." How many times during the latter years of the twentieth century would he repeat those words of Our Lord?

They were words he spoke to the downtrodden and suffering in so many of the countries he visited. They were words he addressed to the people of today in the western world collapsing under materialism and godlessness. They were words which young people in particular responded to - so much so that a whole generation of young Catholics would come to be known as "the John Paul II generation".

A man who came, as he said, "from a far country" made his mark on the modern world's consciousness like no other. A priest, bishop and Supreme Pontiff who sought to bring the men and women of our time to Christ, their true happiness, their true home. A man who world leaders had to respect and listen to, and sometimes feared! A man who came into this life between two world wars, who saw his homeland invaded and occupied first by one foreign atheistic brutal power and then another.

And yet, in the midst of all the hellish torments unleashed in that country in the middle of the twentieth century, some had not forgotten the prophecy of the great Polish romantic poet Juliusz Slowacki. In 1849 he wrote a poem about the Slavic Pope who would be "a brother to all mankind" and who "among the nations with a brother's love spreads the Word".

❧ EARLY LIFE ❧

arol Jozef Wojtyla was born into a free and independent Poland. His father, also Karol Wojtyla, had married Emilia Kaczorowska in 1904 when he was 25 and she was 20. Emilia's father was a saddler who specialised in upholstering horse-drawn carriages at his workshop in Krakow. Emilia is thought to have completed eight grades at a school run by the Sisters of Mercy and after her mother died in 1897 she, of delicate health herself, devoted her time to looking after her father and younger siblings.

From the Heart of Europe

Karol Wojtyla had worked as a tailor before being drafted into the 56th Infantry Regiment of the Austro-Hungarian army in 1900. It is believed that he and Emilia married in the church of Ss Peter and Paul in Krakow's Royal Way, between Wawel Castle and the great market square, which served as the city's military church. Karol was stationed in Krakow on quartermaster duties and the newly-married couple lived in the city for some time until Karol was transferred to Wadowice.

The couple's first child was born in August 1906. Edmund, known in the family as 'Mundek' was a handsome child who became a fine student and athlete and in May 1930 graduated from Krakow's Jagiellonian University as a doctor of medicine. He went on to work in the hospital of Bielsko.

Some years after Edmund's birth, Emilia gave birth to a daughter who died at just a few weeks old.

From 1919 Karol and Emilia lived with Edmund in a second-floor apartment across from the church of St Mary in Wadowice. It was there that the couple's third child and second son was born on 18th May 1920. Having already lost a child in infancy, it must have been a worrying time for the couple as the flu epidemic claimed so many lives worldwide. The child, though, proved to be of robust health! He was baptised by a friend of the family, a military chaplain, in St Mary's Church on 20th June 1920 and given the names Karol Jozef.

In September 1926, the young Karol, now six years old and referred to familiarly as Lolek, began primary school. It was situated on the second floor of the municipal administration building on the town square, just a minute's walk from the Wojtylas' apartment.

Jewish Friends

As a boy Lolek would play in the square with his friends, particularly his close friend Jerzy Kluger who was Jewish. Jews counted for some 2,000 of Wadowice's population. While they had been originally German-speaking, they had become integrated into local society, speaking and dressing as the others, and considered themselves naturally Polish. Jerzy's father, for example, served as an officer in Pilsudski's Polish Legion. In later life John Paul II would remember Jerzy's father, who was a lawyer in civilian life, as a "great Polish patriot".

Lolek and Jerzy with their other boyhood pals would play there in the town square or in each other's homes. In the warm summer months they would swim in the local River Skawa. In winter they would skate on its frozen surface.

Hiking was another favoured pastime, a recreation which Lolek would enjoy for the rest of his life. Many will remember images of him as a septuagenarian pope hiking in the Italian Dolomites!

Soccer was the boys' favourite team sport. Visitors to Wadowice today can still see the field where Lolek usually played in goal, often in a team mostly made up of his Jewish classmates and friends.

In 1927, at the age of seven, Lolek made his First Holy Communion. A surviving photograph shows him looking suitably solemn, his hair freshly cropped, and wearing the white suit of a first communicant.

That same year his father Karol Wojtyla senior, completed his service in the army wherein he had served for 27 years. He retired with the rank of captain and was referred to locally in Wadowice as 'The Captain'.

A Gifted Student

While outside the class-room he took part in the usual games and pranks of schoolboys, inside school Lolek was an attentive and gifted pupil from the start.

Karol Wojtyla in Wadowice in 1932 at the age of twelve.

As he played outside in the courtyard of their building with Jerzy and the others, Emilia Wojtyla would be relieved to see that they were in sight. When he came home from school with some new drawing or handicraft that he had accomplished, Emilia must have been proud of her younger son. No doubt she was pleased that he seemed set to be a bright and dedicated student like his elder brother Edmund.

Tragedy in the Family

However, Emilia was often ill. We do not know how much the young Lolek understood of his mother's increasing illnesses. Perhaps he was somewhat shielded from the harsh realities by being looked after by his friends' families and spending more time at their houses after school and so on.

In 1929, a month before his ninth birthday, there was certainly no escape from the harsh reality for Lolek. His beloved mother died of heart disease and kidney failure. She was buried from St Mary's Church on 16th April 1929. The Captain was left to bring up his two sons on his own, though Edmund was already a man.

That same year of 1930 Lolek moved on from elementary school to the junior section of the all-boys State Secondary School in Wadowice. With Mundek working in Bielsko, except for his visits home, the Captain and ten year-old Lolek developed their own daily routine. School began at 8am and they would rise, say Morning Prayers and breakfast before then. Once Lolek became an altar server, they would very often attend the 7am Mass in St Mary's before school.

Lolek would remember in later life the thrill of going to visit his older brother 'Doctor Mundek' at his hospital in Bielsko. It seems that Mundek encouraged such visits to help take Lolek's mind off the loss of his mother. When Mundek came home to Wadowice on visits, he would take Lolek to soccer games. For his part, when he visited 'Mundek's hospital', Lolek would put on one-man shows for his patients!

Alas, death and separation were to enter Lolek's life again as his beloved brother was stricken with scarlet fever caught from one of his patients. Within days, on 5th December 1932, Mundek died, aged just 26 years.

By now aged twelve and a half, one could almost imagine that the death of his big brother at that age hit Lolek even harder than the death of his beloved mother three and half years before.

On Edmund's gravestone they put that he had "sacrificed his young life in the service of humanity". When friends and neighbours sought to console Lolek on the death of his brother, he spoke to them about it being God's will.

The Domestic Seminary

Now it really was just the Captain and Lolek. They continued with their routine of Morning Prayers and Mass before school. After school, in the early afternoon, they would take their main meal in a café run by Mrs Banas. Her husband was a friend of the Captain's and their son Boguslaw was a friend of Lolek's.

The rest of the afternoon allowed time for homework and some time for play and visiting friends and in the evening the two would eat a light supper prepared by the Captain. Often the two would then take a stroll together around the square.

Friends of Lolek's recounted in later life how as an adolescent and young man, his father was the greatest influence on his life and character.

When he woke in the morning he would see his father on his knees in prayer. At night-time they prayed the Rosary together. His friends also remembered Lolek's father as being a very upright man, a just and honest person, not too severe as might befit an ex-military type, but instead quite approachable and friendly.

In old age, as Pope John Paul II, Karol Wojtyla admitted that he did "not have a clear awareness" of his mother's contribution to his religious training but that it "must have been great".

He did tell the French writer Andre Frossard; "My father was admirable and almost all the memories of my childhood and adolescence are connected with him".

And in his memoirs published for the fiftieth anniversary of his priestly ordination, *Gift and Mystery* John Paul wrote that he was "above all" grateful to his father. "We never spoke about a vocation to the priesthood," he wrote, "but his example was in a way my first seminary, a kind of domestic seminary."

In 1930 a young priest, Father Kazimierz Figlewicz arrived in Wadowice. He would teach catechism in the primary and middle schools and also take responsibility for the altar servers of the parish of St Mary. Lolek went to Father Kazimierz for Confession and the two also became friends outside the confessional and remained in touch when the young priest was later assigned to serve at the Cathedral in Krakow.

At secondary school the young Karol began the study of Latin, a language which he liked and enjoyed for the rest of his life. The following year classical Greek was added to the core subjects of Polish language and literature, history and maths. At home the Captain also gave him and his friend Jerzy private lessons in Polish history.

Further recalling the influence of his father, he recounted in *Rise, let us be on our way*, "From my earliest childhood I have loved books. It was my father who introduced me to reading. He would sit beside me and read to me, for example, Sienkiewicz and other Polish writers. After my mother died, the two of us remained alone. He continued to encourage me to explore good literature and he never stood in the way of my interest in the theatre."

While he continued to master all his school subjects easily, Karol's extra-curricular activities increased. He joined the Sodality of Our Lady and in his final two years at school, was twice elected its president.

As Pope he would recall in *Rise, let us be on our way*, "I have a special devotion to my Guardian Angel. Probably like all children, during my childhood I would often pray, 'Angel of God, my guardian dear, to whom God's love commits me near, ever this day be at my side, to light and guard, to rule and guide.' My Guardian Angel knows what I am doing. My faith in him, in his protective presence, continues to grow deeper and deeper. Saint Michael, Saint

Gabriel, Saint Raphael – these are the archangels I frequently invoke during prayer."

There was a Discalced Carmelite priory outside Wadowice, which the locals referred to as 'the monastery on the hill'. Karol would sometimes make a little pilgrimage there and as a teenager aged 15 he was enrolled in the Brown Scapular of Our Lady of Mount Carmel, which he continued to wear for the rest of his life.

Interest in the Theatre and the Liturgy

At the age of 17, in the summer of 1937, he took part in a compulsory course in 'military preparedness'. A photo shows him very ill-at-ease holding a rifle!

Immersed both at home and at school in Polish literature, the teenage Karol was drawn ever more to the stage. He was becoming more aware of the power not just of a national literature but of the spoken word, and the power of that word proclaimed. One of his mentors was Mieczyslaw Kotlarczyk, who was then teaching history at the girls' high school in Wadowice. Kotlarczyk believed that the actor's task was to so minimise himself that the truth of the spoken word could truly touch the listener. He sought to create a 'theatre of the inner word' in which all the externals of theatrical performance were reduced to the merest minimalism. For him, what mattered was the spoken word.

Karol Wojtyla, appears in a poster for the "Studio 39" theatre

In 1935 Karol's school and the girls' school produced the ancient Greek play *Antigone*, in which Karol performed.

In 1937 the two schools produced a play in which Karol ended up playing two parts, having had to learn the second overnight after the pupil playing the part got himself suspended from school! Along with that production, they put on three other plays during that academic year of 1937-38. The performances were so appreciated that the youthful theatre company went on tour, taking the works to other amateur theatres in the region. His friends appreciated that Karol had a talent for acting and many expected him to pursue a career in the theatre. The parish of St Mary also put on dramatic works in which Karol performed.

When he was 15, Karol was invited by his old friend, the young priest Father Figlewicz who had been transferred to the cathedral at Krakow, to come and take part in the Sacred Triduum at Wawel Cathedral. Nearly 70 years later he would write; "The Liturgy is also a kind of acted *mysterium*, played out on stage. I remember the deep emotion I felt when... I was present for the Tenebrae Services... It was a profound spiritual experience for me..."

In that final year at school, as well as preparing for leaving exams and seeking entrance to university, and performing in (and directing) several plays, Karol prepared for the Sacrament of Confirmation, which he received on 3rd May 1938.

On 27th May that year Karol and his classmates graduated from secondary school. At the graduation ball held with the local girls' school, the young group of friends danced until late. It was the end of a stage in their lives. They also knew that a new more sinister time was dawning in their beloved Poland.

Anti-Semitism Grows

In 1935 Marshal Jozef Pilsudski, the towering figure of the Second Polish Republic, died. Anti-semitism began to appear in Poland and boycotts of Jewish businesses were organised. In 1938 Jerzy Kluger saw that his father had added his Hebrew name to his office nameplate, a requirement of a new law. During their last year at school Karol and Jerzy saw some of their friends join anti-semitic political parties. Karol always defended the Jews and argued with his classmates that to be anti-Semitic was to be anti-Christian.

One night a mob had stoned the business premises and homes of some local Jews. The next day in a public act of solidarity Karol's father, the Captain, was waiting outside as school ended. As Karol and Jerzy Kruger strolled over to greet him, the retired officer gave Jerzy a rough hug and asked how he was. In a loud voice he continued, "How is your dear father? Please do give him my regards. Don't forget now, do you hear me? Give your father my very best regards."

Another Jewish friend of Karol and Jerzy's through their dramatic activities with Kotlarczyk, Ginka Beer, was by 1938 at medical school in Krakow. A disciplinary charge was trumped up to drive her out of medical school. Everyone knew it was an anti-semitic action. She decided to get out of Poland and to head for a new life in Palestine. Karol and Jerzy visited her before she left. She told them, "What is happening to Jews in Germany, will happen here too. I've decided to leave." She later recalled that as she was leaving Wadowice they walked her to the railway station. The Captain also accompanied them and said to Ginka, "Not all Poles are anti-Semitic. You know that I'm not!" She was struck by the fact that her friend the eighteen-year old Karol was too upset even to speak.

Move to Krakow and University

In his final year at senior secondary school Karol was proclaimed dux or school captain. As such it fell to him to pronounce a speech of welcome when the Archbishop of Krakow, Prince Adam Sapieha, visited the school. The Archbishop asked the chaplain of the Sodality of Mary if this brilliant student was likely to become a priest? No, it was not likely, replied the priest, as Karol Wojtyla was going off to the Jagiellonian University to study literature and language.

That summer of 1938 the two Karols, father and son, moved from Wadowice to Krakow. They took up residence in the basement flat of a house built by Lolek's uncle and Karol senior's brother-in-law, the brother of Emilia, at the end of the First World War. Two of Emilia's sisters still lived on the upper floors. The basement flat was small, and somewhat dark and damp. The location was fine though! The house was situated in the Debniki district of Krakow, on the south bank of the River Vistula, and one could look across at the fine view of Wawel Castle and cathedral. Karol had just a twenty-minute walk to reach his courses at the university, across the Debniki Bridge and into the Old Town. He threw himself into undergraduate life at one of Europe's oldest and most venerable universities.

As well as a full range of courses to do with language and letters, he took private lessons in French. He also did volunteer work as a librarian in the university and took part in several student poetry societies. Karol became a member too of the Circle of Scholars of Polish Studies. Among other things it resisted the restrictions on Jews studying at the university.

Karol's friend Jerzy had gone to Warsaw to study engineering. Already in the autumn of 1938 there was an outburst of violent anti-semitism there and Jerzy retreated to his home town of Wadowice.

In Krakow Karol and his friends continued to throw themselves into student life. On top of his full schedule, Karol was informed that as part of the national military service he must attend PE classes two evenings a week, Tuesdays and Fridays from 8pm to 9pm.

Once again, in 1939, the teenage Karol was able to attend the Holy Week services at the cathedral, where the venerable Prince-Archbishop went on bended knee and washed feet just as the Lord had done. In May of that year Karol took part in a student pilgrimage to Czestochowa. Who could have thought that one day millions of young people would gather there to be with him as John Paul II?

For now, as a student, Karol immersed himself in the subjects he so loved. He later wrote, "As a university student I read many different authors. First I turned to literature, especially plays. I read Shakespeare, Moliere, the Polish poets Norwid, Wyspianski, and, of course, Aleksander Fredrom. My greatest love, however was acting, appearing on stage, and I often wondered which characters I would like to play. Kotlarczyk and I would amuse ourselves by assigning roles to each other and wondering who could best play a particular part."

Nazi Occupation

The 1st September 1939 was a Friday. As was his custom, Karol went to the cathedral early in the morning to make his first Friday confession and serve Fr Figlewicz's Mass. [In the 17th century Our Lord had asked St Margaret Mary Alacoque that we go to Mass and Confession on the First Friday of the month in honour of his Sacred Heart.] During the peace and quiet, the early-morning stillness of that Holy Mass, the air-raid sirens went off. Then there was the buzz of the Luftwaffe planes followed by the sound of exploding bombs.

The little congregation ran for their lives. Priest and altar server continued to the conclusion of Holy Mass. Then Karol told his priest friend. "I've got to go. Dad's at home on his own."

The occupying Nazi power soon made its presence felt in every area of life. Parts of Poland, including Wadowice, were immediately annexed into the Third Reich. The rest would be governed by the Nazi Hans Franck who installed himself in Krakow's Wawel Castle. He wrote, "The Pole has no rights whatsoever. His only obligation is to obey what we tell him. A major goal of our plan is to finish off as speedily as possible all troublemaking politicians, priests and leaders who fall into our hands."

The Nazi aim was to obliterate the Polish nation, the Polish identity. The Poles' "obligation to obey" the Nazi oppressor was swiftly enacted. There were two punishments for any category of perceived crime or 'disobedience' – you were sent to a concentration camp or you were shot on the spot.

Of all the countries invaded by Nazi Germany, Poland was the only one in which they could not even establish a semblance of a collaborationist government. The legitimate Polish government fled into exile along with the Primate, Cardinal Hlond, eventually establishing itself in London. A brave and determined Polish resistance movement grew up, linked to the government-in-exile.

Franck closed down Wawel Cathedral, symbol of Polish history, culture, religion, its very identity – later allowing Father Figlewicz to offer two Holy Masses a week there, under the supervision of armed German guards.

In May 1941 the Salesian priest Father Jozef Kowalski was arrested from the Wojtylas' local parish at Debniki. At Auschwitz when he refused to grind Rosary beads under his foot he was drowned in human excrement. The prior of the Discalced Carmelite priory at Czerna was taken from his monastery and beaten to death. The former prior of the Carmelite priory in Krakow died at Dachau in 1945 from typhus caught while voluntarily serving the camp's sick. The Bishop of Wloclawek, Michael Kozal, died at Dachau in 1943. More than 3,500 Polish priests were sent to concentration camps and over 2,500 of them were killed.

Escape

As Krakow was being invaded, Karol and his father decided to leave the city. They joined the thousands upon thousands of others who began heading east. The Captain was already failing in health and he would occasionally need to ride along on the back of a cart. Karol, like so many others, walked. They had made it as far as the San River, some 120 miles from Krakow, when they learned that the Red Army of the Russians had invaded Poland from the east. What to do? Faced with summary execution or capture and deportation to Soviet Russia by the Reds, they decided to head back to Krakow occupied by the Nazis. At least they had a roof over their heads there. They turned heel and began the long walk home.

When they got there, they found the Nazi swastika flying over Wawel Castle. In the city there were shops "for Germans only". Only in those was to be found meat, fresh vegetables, butter. Poles, on the other hand, would have to start queueing even from 4am to buy a lump of black bread. In a letter to Kotlarczyck, still living in Wadowice, Karol wrote, "Life in Krakow …consists of standing in line for bread, or (rare) expeditions to find sugar." The young intellectual missed acutely the relatively carefree days when once he and his friends could read and discuss late into the night. "For us, life once consisted of refined conversation, of dreams and longings. We dreamt away many an evening until midnight or beyond, but now…"

He and his friends, though, did continue to meet in secret to read classic Polish texts and plays and Karol wrote two plays himself. His father the Captain supported his son's efforts and they all risked deportation or worse if caught.

The ancient Jagiellonian university kept to its centuries-old tradition of opening its doors for the Michaelmas Term in October. Aware that things would be unlikely to continue as they once had, many lecturers began teaching early, before the academic year had officially begun.

A lecture to all academic staff by an SS commander was announced for the 6th November 1939. Some, being suspicious, failed to turn up. But 184 academics did attend. They were soon rounded up and deported to Sachenshausen concentration camp, where many of them would die. The Nazis then went on a spree of destruction, looting libraries, wrecking laboratories and lecture halls.

Karol continued "to do a lot of reading and writing". In fact by early 1942 the Jagiellonian had an underground university up and running. Its lecturers and professors risked their lives by continuing to teach their students in secret get-togethers, often in private homes at night-time.

The Quarry

In order to avoid deportation to do forced labour in Germany, for the first year of the war Karol had worked as a store messenger for a restaurant. As the occupiers tightened up their rules about work, in the autumn of 1940 Karol began work in a stone quarry. It was attached to the Solvay chemical plant about half an hour's walk from his home in Debniki. He would work at this manual labour for nearly four years.

Once he witnessed the death of a fellow-worker. During the detonation of a dynamite charge some rocks struck and killed the man. That experience left a deep impression on Karol and he wrote about it in a poem; "They took his body and walked in a silent line. Toil still lingered about him, a sense of wrong."

Karol's father, the Captain, became weaker as the war continued. By Christmas 1940, aged 61, he was bedridden.

Alone

One freezing day in February 1941 Karol came home from the quarry to find his father dead in bed. His friend Julius Kydrynski came to be with him as he kept watch all that night and prayed for his father's soul. Despite his friend's company, Karol later confessed that he had never in his life felt so alone. A few days later Karol's friend Father Figlewicz offered the Requiem Mass and the Captain was buried in the military section of a local cemetery.

Julius' family invited Karol to come and live with them, an offer he accepted. The death of his beloved father obviously had a profound effect on the 19 year-old Karol, and Julius later remembered that Karol would pray while prostrate on the floor, arms stretched out in the shape of the Cross.

The Living Rosary

In May of 1941 the Salesian priests who ran Karol's local parish of St Stanislaw at Debniki were arrested by the Gestapo, many of them to perish in concentration camps. The Salesians had run a flourishing youth apostolate, which the Nazis looked on with suspicion. Knowing that they could be rounded up at any time, the religious had encouraged responsible lay people to help in this work with the parish's young people. One of these was Jan Tyranowski. The 34 year-old tailor lived a devout and ascetic spiritual life and had founded an association of young men called *The Living Rosary*. Four assistant leaders, answerable to Tyranowski, each led a group of 15 youngsters. Wojtyla was one of these four leaders. Tyranowski's living out of the Gospel in his everyday life had a large influence on Karol and it was the devout tailor who introduced him to the writings of the Carmelite mystic St John of the Cross. Aware of Karol's dramatic and poetic works, perhaps Tyranowski reasoned that the saint's poems would resonate with the 20 year-old Polish lover of literature and drama.

Karol's understanding of Marian devotion grew and developed during this time too. While he had been much involved in the Sodality of Mary at senior school, he later went through a short period in which, as he later explained, he tried to have a more 'adult' relationship with Christ himself, directly, somehow seeking less mediation on the part of Our Lady. While he was working at the quarry and the chemical plant the Polish foremen and other labourers made allowances for their young intellectual to keep up with his reading, particularly during night-shifts. Thus it was that Karol read the works of the 17th-century French saint, Louis Grignon de Montfort, and in particular his *True Devotion to the Blessed Virgin Mary*. This pointed out that *true* devotion to Mary always led to Christ.

Karol moved back to his own apartment in Debniki and took in his friends the dramatist Mieczyslaw Kotlarczyk and his wife Zofia when they escaped from Wadowice and came to Krakow in July 1941. Mieczyslaw took work as a tram driver and in the August founded the clandestine *Theatre of the Living Word*. Karol would write some sixty years later: "Sharing the same house, we were able not only to continue our conversations about the theatre, but also to attempt some actual performances…

"It was essential to keep these theatrical get-togethers secret; otherwise we risked serious punishment from the occupying forces, even deportation to the concentration camps. I must admit that that whole experience of the theatre left a deep impression on me, even though at a certain point I came to realise that this was not my real vocation."

❧ FATHER WOJTYLA ❧

Wh**ile he began to sense that the Lord was calling him to a vocation other than the theatre, it would take over a year before Karol would be completely sure and take concrete action.

In October 1941 he transferred from the quarry to the Solvay chemical plant. He would carry buckets of lime attached to a wooden yoke which lay over his shoulders.

Vocation

As he read St Louis de Montfort and St John of the Cross in his workplace, even some of his colleagues would say to him, "You know Karol, you should be a priest."

Kotlarczyk's *Theatre of the Living Word* gave its first clandestine performance on the evening of 1st November 1941, with Karol playing the leading role.

As he and the others were well aware, such activities would be viewed as highly subversive by the occupying Germans and the participants risked deportation or summary execution. The young intellectuals, though, even in the midst of the most cruel and humiliating occupation by a foreign power, were determined to hold on to their human dignity and their national identity. Just as with the *Living Rosary Group* they would talk and plan how life would one day be when Poland would be free again. From 1940 and his participation in the *Rhapsodic Theatre Group* Karol had been involved in a wider underground organisation which linked many such resistance groups. It was called simply UNIA (Union in Polish). It sought to lay the foundations of what kind of society Poland would be when one day it would be free from totalitarian domination. It looked to the day when Poland would again rule itself, and run its economic and social life in conformity with the Social Teaching of the Church.

While its military resistance component trained people to join a Polish Home Army, its Council to Help the Jews helped thousands of Jews to escape capture and deportation.

It also sponsored a Cultural Union which as well as organising underground lectures and discussions published an underground newspaper.

Unia, then, sought to guard and promote all that was noble and held society together, all that was good in the true Polish identity, the identity the occupier wanted to crush and destroy. Another 'union', called simply *Solidarity*, would pursue the same ends under domination by another power, the Communists, over forty years later.

The Final Decision

Karol obviously discussed his growing realisation of a religious vocation with his closest friends. He said in later life that Mieczyslaw Kotlarczyk spent days trying to dissuade him, saying, "What are you doing? Do you want to waste your (theatrical) talents?"

In the autumn of 1942 Karol made what he called "my final decision to enter the Krakow seminary, which was operating clandestinely". The Rector accepted him as a secret seminarian with the warning that not even those dearest to him must know about it.

He recounted in *Gift and Mystery* how "faced with the spread of evil and the atrocities of the war, the meaning of the priesthood and its mission in the world became much clearer to me." The invasion by the Germans, the closure of his beloved university and the loss of his much-loved father all brought with them, he said, "a progressive detachment" from his earlier plans. But it was not just a negative process. "At the same time a light was beginning to shine ever more brightly in the back of my mind: *the Lord wants me to become a priest.* One day I saw this with great clarity; it was like an interior illumination which brought with it the joy and certainty of a new vocation. And this awareness filled me with great inner peace."

First Encounters with Theology

Karol continued to live in his apartment at Debniki and to work at the Solvay chemical plant. He later recalled, "As a clandestine seminarian, I was given the manual on metaphysics... Father Klosak said, 'Study this! When you've learnt it you'll take the exam.' For a few months I immersed myself in the text. I took the exam and I passed. This was a turning point in my life – a whole new world opened up before me. I began to engage with theological books…"

The first two years of seminary, devoted to the study of philosophy, Karol completed while still working as a labourer at the chemical plant. The next two years, 1944 and 1945, as he later wrote, saw him "become increasingly involved at the Jagiellonian University, even though the programme of studies was very incomplete that first year following the war. The 1945-46 academic year, however, was normal."

An Accident

As he was walking home from a double shift at the chemical works on 29th February 1944, Karol was knocked down by a German lorry. A woman travelling on a tram spotted the body of the young worker lying by the roadside and jumped off to help. He was unconscious and bleeding. A German officer saw the woman tending a body at the roadside and stopped his car. Seeing that the young labourer was still alive, the officer flagged down a passing timber lorry and sent Karol to hospital. When Karol came to he found himself in hospital with a bandaged head and his arm in plaster. He had suffered severe concussion and a shoulder injury. He would be left with a noticeable stoop of his left shoulder.

A close escape

The 1st of August 1944 saw the Warsaw Uprising. On Sunday 6th August the Gestapo made a sweep of Krakow. They sought to round up the young men in order to avoid a similar uprising taking place there. When the Gestapo called at Karol's residence, they searched the two upper floors. In his basement flat he hid behind a door, barely daring to breathe. For one reason or another, the soldiers never thought to search the basement!

When he could (depending on his shifts at the works), Karol the secret seminarian would go to the Archbishop's house in the morning to serve at Holy Mass. One morning, while recovering from his accident, he arrived as usual to serve at the Archbishop's Mass but his fellow clandestine seminarian who was due to serve with him did not turn up. After Mass Karol went to Jerzy Zachuta's house only to discover that the Gestapo had come during the night and taken him away. Jerzy was executed.

The Seminary Moves to the Archbishop's Residence

Archbishop Adam Stefan Sapieha was right to be worried for the other students of his secret seminary. In the early days of the occupation the seminary was closed down. The Archbishop decided, therefore, to assign his seminarians to different parishes. They would come together for meetings and courses as circumstances would allow. But even this dispersal had not been enough to guarantee their safety and five of the young men had been taken by the Gestapo and either shot or sent to concentration camps. It was after this that the archbishop instituted his policy of complete clandestinity, the students continuing to live at home, keep their regular jobs and study in secret. Karol was one of the first group of ten to begin this programme.

After the Gestapo sweep of Krakow, the archbishop could sense that things were hotting up. He moved the seminarians into his own residence. Upon arrival they were each given a cassock. If the house were raided, the archbishop would explain that these young clerics were his secretaries! Karol's old friend from his time in Wadowice, Father Figlewicz, still attached to the cathedral, was called upon to use his contacts. He spoke to the works foreman at the Solvay chemical plant. One way or another, despite the risks to himself, the foreman managed to make Karol Wojtyla's name 'disappear' from the works list.

From September 1944 Karol lived and studied with his fellow seminarians in the archbishop's house. With them were a priest as rector of the seminary and a young priest who had studied for a doctorate in Rome as their spiritual director. Despite living in the midst of the evil that was being unleashed on them, the archbishop knew that he also had to prepare for the future. While his priests were being shot or shipped off to die in concentration camps, while he gave the order that baptismal certificates were to be issued to Jews to save them from deportation, while parishes were to be organised to get some sustenance secretly to those suffering in Nazi labour camps by leaving food packages in nearby woods, all the while the archbishop planned for the future too. To rebuild a ravaged Church and society, Poland would need good and strong and holy priests.

When his little band of secret seminarians arrived at his residence he told them; he was not prepared NOT to train young men to minister to Christ's people in the future. He did not hold any hope of the Nazis giving permission to reopen his seminary so he would establish it right here in his house. The Lord would look after them.

A drawing room became their dormitory. Each one had a bed and any few belongings a seminarian had with him were kept in a suitcase or box under his bed; there was simply no room or cupboard to put things anywhere else. Another drawing room served as the classroom. A full daily schedule was organised for the seminary, beginning with private prayer from 6am and Mass at 7am, followed by a meagre breakfast. Classes were then held until the noon Angelus and lunch. The afternoon was devoted to private study, interrupted by a period of Eucharistic adoration at 3pm. The spiritual director or the archbishop gave a spiritual talk at 6.30, before dinner at 7pm. At 8.15 the group gathered in the chapel again for night prayer and private devotions. Instinctively the seminarians knew to leave the archbishop alone with his Lord when Sapieha retired to the chapel at 9 o'clock each evening for an hour's adoration. During the course of each day he tried to exchange a word with each of his seminarians. By the time it came to ordaining them, they were candidates whom the ordaining bishop knew very well indeed!

Liberation!

On the bitter-cold night of 17th-18th January, the occupying German forces withdrew in the face of the advancing Red Army. As they left, the Germans blew up Debniki bridge. Karol later wrote: "I remember that terrible explosion; the blast broke all the windows of the archbishop's residence. At that moment we were in the chapel for a ceremony with the Archbishop. The following day we worked quickly to repair the damage."

Soon after repairing the windows, the students went to reclaim the diocese's seminary building near Wawel Castle, which the SS had occupied. It was a disaster area! The roof had collapsed, the windows were shattered. The central heating system no longer worked and open fires had been lit in the middle of rooms. The lavatories had become open-plan latrines and piles of frozen excrement had to be chopped up and carted away. Karol and fellow student Mieczyslaw Malinski volunteered for this horrible task before setting to work on restoring the roof.

Poland's 'liberation' turned out to be anything but. Sold out by the Allies at Yalta, Soviet domination would be its lot for the next forty-odd years.

The Jagiellonian University emerged from clandestinity. Karol Wojtyla was elected vice president of the Students' Fraternal Aid Society. This was an organisation that helped to distribute aid arriving from the West. Karol's fellow students and fellow seminarians could see that he continued to live in poverty himself, by choice. When his friend the dramatist Mieczyslaw Kotlarczyk sent him a new jumper, Karol gave it away to a beggar who had arrived asking to see him personally.

Sapieha made Cardinal

For a year Karol continued his studies at the once-more legal university and at seminary. He completed his preordination theology studies by passing all his exams at the end of June and the beginning of July 1946. Before that, though, he and his fellow students had the joy of a celebration in February. The new Pope, Pius XII, made Prince-Archbishop Adam Sapieha a cardinal. When he returned from receiving his red hat in Rome, the cardinal's train was met at Krakow station by a crowd of students. Sapieha was a national hero, the symbol of Poland's true identity during the long years of Nazi occupation. When he sat in his car outside the railway station, the students simply lifted it up and carried it all the way to St Mary's church in the Old Town market square!

At a celebration with the cardinal in the seminary, Karol Wojtyla proclaimed a reading. It was a homily written by a 19th-century Polish priest hero on the religious meaning of true patriotism.

Early Ordination

Cardinal Sapieha wanted Wojtyla to have an experience of the Universal Church in Rome and so he decided that his outstanding seminarian should go to the Eternal City to begin his doctoral studies. First, though, he would be ordained priest ahead of schedule. His fellow seminarians of the underground group would be ordained on Palm Sunday of the following year.

The month of October 1946 was in fact an extended period of retreat for Karol as first he made a six-day retreat before being ordained to the subdiaconate, then another retreat before being ordained a deacon. Finally, he made another six-day retreat before his priestly ordination which was scheduled for 1st November, the feast of All Saints, 1946.

That day, in the chapel of the Archbishop's residence, Karol Wojtyla was ordained to the sacred priesthood. Five years ago to the day he had been reading in the first performance of Kotlarczyk's underground theatre group.

The Church's entire theology of the sacred priesthood was summed up in the final blessing the Archbishop gave the new priest at the end of the ceremony: "The blessing of God Almighty, the Father, the Son, and the Holy Spirit, descend upon you; that you may be blessed in the Priestly Order and may offer propitiatory sacrifices for the sins and offences of the people to Almighty God, to whom belongs glory and honour, world without end."

The only living blood relative of Karol's to attend the ordination ceremony was his late mother's elder sister, his own aunt and godmother. Karol thought especially that day of his "brother in the priestly vocation" who should have been ordained with him, Jerzy Zachuta, who had been killed by the Gestapo.

The post-war circumstances did not provide any means to print the traditional memoriam cards of his ordination or first Mass. Instead Karol simply wrote on the back of some pious cards, in his own neat hand, the phrase from Mary's Magnificat, "Fecit mihi magna... Krakow, 1st Nov 1946": "He has done great things for me…"

While still studying at the clandestine seminary, Karol had approached the archbishop … in fact, he considered that he might have a vocation to Carmel, to join the Discalced Carmelite fathers. The Archbishop responded in his typical direct way, "First you have to finish what you have begun." That is, he had begun a programme of formation to be ordained a priest of the diocese of Krakow. And that is what he completed!

The day following Karol's ordination was the 2nd November, All Souls' Day when the whole Church focuses on praying for the deceased and enters the month of the Holy Souls, before embarking upon a new liturgical year with the season of Advent.

On All Souls' day every Catholic priest may offer the sacrifice of Holy Mass three times. Father Karol chose to offer his Holy Masses in the crypt chapel of St Leonard in Wawel Cathedral. He chose this location to express his "special spiritual bond with the history of Poland" as so many kings, queens, bishops, cardinals and poets were buried there.

Wearing the black vestments proper to Requiem Masses according to the traditional liturgy of the Church, and with a few friends present, young Father Karol offered his first Masses for the repose of the souls of his mother, his father and his brother.

Rome

The new young priest and the fresh young seminarian left Krakow on 15th November, heading for Katowice where they joined the train for Paris. In the 'city of light' they spent a few nights at the Polish seminary. Shortly afterwards they left Paris for Rome. For a few weeks they lodged with the Pallotine Fathers before taking up residence where the Cardinal had arranged for them, at the Belgian college. In the immediate post-war period things were basic. The British military had installed indoor toilets in the Belgian College, and some showers had just been installed that year. The little rooms were basic; a bed, a table and chair and a sink. But Karol was happy. Here he was at the heart of holy Mother Church, the city of the Apostles Peter and Paul, the very centre of Christendom where the successor of Peter governed the Church to this day.

Father Karol was to complete his doctoral studies at the Angelicum, so-called after its patron, the angelic doctor; it is officially the Pontifical Athenaeum of St Thomas

Aquinas. On his way to the Angelicum he would stop off to say a prayer in the church of Sant'Andrea del Quirinale, which contained the relics of St Stanislaw Kostka, the 16th-century Jesuit saint, patron of Polish youth, and patron of his home parish at Debniki in Krakow.

The two years spent in Rome would also allow Father Karol and his young colleague from the Diocese of Krakow to visit other parts of 'western' Europe.

Padre Pio

From Rome, however, he went first to San Giovanni Rotondo during the Easter holidays of 1947. There he went to confession to the famous Capuchin stigmatist Padre Pio. It would not be his last contact with Padre Pio!

[Incidentally, after being elected Pope in 1978, rumours began to circulate that Padre Pio had prophesied this to the young priest during that brief encounter in the confessional of 1947. In the mid-1980s while visiting a Capuchin-run parish in Rome, John Paul II told the superior-general of the Capuchin Order that the rumours were not true. Instead he remembered Padre Pio as being very simple, brief and direct as a confessor.]

Padre Pio lived most of his priestly life as a 'prisoner of the confessional'.

The Curé d'Ars

Another famous priest to have done so was the 19th-century French country priest St John Vianney, the Cure d'Ars. After visiting France and Holland during the summer holidays of 1947, Father Karol acted as supply chaplain for a month to the Polish community of miners and their families in the Belgian town of Charleroi. On his way back to Rome he stopped off at Ars where St John Vianney had exercised his ministry and had been also a 'prisoner of the confessional'. The days spent in Ars had a deep effect on the young Polish priest. He later recalled, "That humble priest, who would hear confessions more than ten hours a day, eating little and sleeping only a few hours was able, at a difficult moment in history, to inspire a kind of spiritual revolution in France, and not only there. Thousands of people passed through Ars and knelt at his confessional. Against the background of attacks on the Church and the clergy in the nineteenth century, his witness was truly revolutionary.

"My encounter with this saintly figure confirmed me in the conviction that a priest fulfils an essential part of his mission through the confessional – by voluntarily 'making himself a prisoner in the confessional'."

And so Father Karol, soon to celebrate the first anniversary of his own ordination, headed back to Rome filled with thoughts of priestly spirituality. At theAngelicum he was preparing his own doctoral thesis on 'The Doctrine of Faith according to St John of the Cross' under the direction of Father Garrigou-Lagrange. He had already started to read the works of the Spanish mystic after being introduced to them at home in Poland by Jan Tyranowski and had taught himself Spanish so as to be able to read them in the original. Tyranowski, who had been ill for some time, died in March of 1947.

Doctorate

On 14th June 1948 Father Karol passed his doctoral exams with 18 marks out of a possible 20. At the beginning of July his oral defence of his dissertation earned him the maximum 50 marks out of a possible 50!

However, the brilliant young Polish priest did not receive a doctorate from the Angelicum as the convention was that one could not receive a doctorate until one's work had been published. This young Polish priest in the post-war years of hardship did not have the means to publish his dissertation and so he departed Rome having passed his exams with flying colours, but with no doctorate!

At home in Poland he submitted his work to the Theology Faculty of the Jagiellonian University and after examination there he was awarded a doctorate of theology by that university in December 1948.

Many years later, as Pope, Wojtyla once again expressed his thanks to the members of the Belgian College who had been his hosts during those two academic years in Rome, and particulary to the rector, Father de Furstenberg. He also recalled how during the conclave of 1978 the then Cardinal de Furstenberg came up to him and whispered the words of the Apostle Andrew to his brother Peter, "*Dominus adest et vocat te*": "the Lord is here and he is calling you..."

As Pope, he later testified that he left Rome with "not only a much broader theological education but also a strengthened priesthood and a more profound vision of the Church. ...in Rome the early years of my priesthood had taken on both a European and a universal dimension. I returned from Rome to Krakow with that sense of the universality of the priestly mission..."

First Posting

The moment he arrived in Krakow, he went straight to the Archdiocesan Curia to receive his first 'posting'. Archbishop Sapieha himself had gone to Rome at that moment but had left instructions for the returning Father Karol. He would serve as curate in the country parish of Niegowic. Returning from the 'capital' of Roman Catholicism, the young priestly heart delighted at the prospect of serving God's people in a Polish country village. Thereafter he remembered vividly his arrival in his 'first parish'. "I went from Krakow to Gdow by bus, and from there a local man gave me a ride in his cart to the village of Marszowice; from there he advised me to take a short-cut through the fields on foot. …When I finally reached the territory of Niegowic parish, I knelt down and kissed the ground. It was a gesture I had learned from St John Mary Vianney. In the church I made a visit to the Blessed Sacrament and then introduced myself to the parish priest."

A Life lived in Poverty

The villager who gave the new young curate a ride in his cart, like the other parishioners, could not help but notice the poverty of their new priest. His sum worldly possessions, his Missal, his Breviary, a few other books and a change of clothes, were contained in a battered little suitcase. The young padre's cassock had seen better days and was somewhat threadbare. Sometime in his teenage years, probably since the experience of the invasion of his beloved homeland and his initial trek as a refugee with his ageing father, Karol Wojtyla had determined to live his life in evangelical poverty. He would do so for the rest of his days even as Pope he had no personal possessions to leave in his will.

At Niegowic he was put in charge of the five primary schools in the villages which formed the parish. Villagers would take him to the different schools by horse or mule-drawn cart. The young priest would recite his Breviary in Latin as he bumped along the country lanes and then enjoy some conversation with his 'driver' until they reached their destination.

Back to Krakow and University Chaplaincy

From Niegowic he was transferred in March 1949 to the city centre parish of Saint Florian in Krakow. The parish priest entrusted him with teaching catechism to the senior classes of the secondary school. He was also to provide pastoral care to the students of the university. While the university chaplaincy had been based at St Anne's parish in Krakow, the addition of new university faculties necessitated the creation of a new centre at St Florian's. Every Thursday Father Karol would give talks to the students on fundamental problems concerning the existence of God and the spiritual nature of the human soul. As he later recalled, "These were extremely important issues, given the militant atheism being promoted by the communist regime." Soon the texts of Fr Karol's talks were being typed up, mimeographed and circulated clandestinely as samizdat publications.

Communist Pressure

Already in 1947 the communists had formed the 'Pax' movement as they did in other countries they occupied, in an attempt to undermine the Church. In 1950 Catholic schools, the Catholic Action organisation and other Catholic organisations were declared illegal.

The Communists, as they had done since the first days of the Bolshevik revolution in Russia, sought to undermine the family in every way. Children were to be kept away from their parents as much as possible; for example, work shifts for the adults would begin an hour or so before school started so that the children would have to be entrusted to state-run nurseries or crèches. Husbands and wives would have to work different shifts so that the family was rarely all together. Social housing was built too small so that a normal family life with several children became a problem.

Father Karol did all he could to engage the young students of Krakow in serious reflection about the Faith and the fundamental nature of the human person. While the German National-Socialists (Nazis) had proclaimed that 'work makes you free', for the Communists the human person was just another cog in the great collective. Only the Catholic Church has consistently proclaimed that the human person is of intrinsic value and dignity, each individual made in the image and likeness of God.

Not only students but older members of the intelligentsia began to flock to hear the young priest's sermons. Each year he produced a series of 'mystery plays' in the parish. Whereas Gregorian plainchant tended to be restricted to monasteries, Father Karol set up a choir and got the parish singing the Gregorian chants at Sunday Mass. He also encouraged the young people to use their Missals and even initiated so-called 'dialogue Masses' where the people would recite the responses normally reserved to those serving at the priest's side in the sanctuary.

Ministry to Young People and Couples

In those days couples intending to marry in a Catholic church might only meet the priest once in advance to arrange the details and fill in the necessary paperwork. In 1950 Father Karol launched the first marriage preparation course. In 1951 the Cardinal added a chaplaincy to the city's health-care workers to Fr Karol's responsibilities. From then on he invited lay professionals, doctors, nurses and psychologists to help lead the marriage preparation programme.

With his young people, the group that had started out as the little choir to learn plainchant, Father Karol reached out to those who were sick or lonely. He encouraged the youngsters to invite others to join them at his Thursday night talks or his early Wednesday morning Mass. Then they began to meet in smaller groups in private homes where they might finally trust each other with their family names. In fact, the group forming around the dynamic Father Karol was like an antidote to the normal atmosphere in the university and wider society where people were afraid of the ever-present communist spies and snitches.

Call me Uncle

Around Father Karol they felt completely at home and came to call themselves 'the little family'. Once when they were going on a day-trip to the country, to avoid attracting the notice of the communist authorities, Father Karol dressed in some old and worn plain clothes rather than his usual threadbare cassock. One of the young girls foresaw a problem. While travelling on the train with this disguised priest, they couldn't very well continue to call him 'Father'. Quoting a famous Polish play, Karol replied, 'Call me Uncle'. And so to Krakow's young people he became 'Uncle'.

Academia

In July 1951 the Prince–Cardinal, Archbishop Adam Sepieha of Krakow, died. The man who had symbolised resistance first under the Nazi yoke and then under communist oppression was laid in state in Wawel Cathedral before being buried next to the tomb of Saint Stanislaw.

His successor Archbishop Baziak had lived and worked with Cardinal Sapieha, since the latter took him in after he was expelled from his own diocese of Lwow when that had been made part of the Soviet Republic of Ukraine.

Baziak decided that Fr Karol would undertake further academic work. Karol was not favourable to the idea – he had got so much going on with all his work at St Florian's with young people, students, health professionals, families. Baziak had very likely discussed the plan with Cardinal Sapieha before he died and in any case, of course Wojtyla submitted in total obedience. But the decision cost him. He admitted years later, "This meant that I would have less time for the pastoral work so dear to me. This was a sacrifice, but from that time on I was always resolved that my dedication to the study of theology and philosophy would not lead me to 'forget' that I was a priest; rather it would help me to become one ever more fully."

Father Karol was given a two-year sabbatical to prepare a habilitation thesis which would qualify him to lecture in ethics and moral theology. No doubt aware of the young priest's propensity to work 18-hour days and his constant reaching out to people, particularly young people and families, Archbishop Baziak decreed that any apostolic work on Karol's part must be approved by him. He also moved him out of St Florian's and into another Church property known as the Dean's house. It would remain his home for the next six years. Another priest, Father Rozycki lived there and it was he who suggested the topic for Karol's habilitation thesis on Max Scheler's book *Der Formalismus in der Ethik und materiale Wertethik*. The two priests became lifelong friends.

Father Karol defended his thesis in November 1953 and his was the last habilitation granted by the faculty of theology at the Jagiellonian before it was suppressed by the communist authorities.

University Teaching

One of the three academics who were the readers of Karol's habilitation thesis was Stefan Swiezawski. One day in September 1954 Swiezawski and his wife were hiking with Father Karol in the hills outside Krakow. Stefan urged the young philosopher priest as forcefully as he could to join the academic staff of Lublin University.

This Catholic university had been founded in 1918 and it had been given a state charter by the Second Polish Republic in 1938. As this state charter had never been revoked, the little Catholic university had been able to continue functioning during the Nazi occupation and now during the communist domination.

While they did not close it down, the communists certainly did not make life easy for the Catholic University of Lublin or its staff, its students and its graduates.

Swiezawski, for example, while lecturing in philosophy at Lublin, could not obtain a transfer from Krakow and was forced to commute to Lublin, spending hours travelling between the two cities.

After the experience of the Second World War and the Nazi occupation and brutality, Lublin created its own faculty of philosophy.

Father Karol had begun lecturing in social ethics at the Jagiellonian University in October 1953. When the communists closed the faculty down in 1954 he transferred his course to the school of theology that was set up for the seminarians who now had no university theology courses to attend.

When he gave in to Swiezawski's insistence in September 1954, a philosophy faculty meeting of Lublin University soon appointed Father Karol Wojtyla to teach his courses there.

Every fortnight Father Karol would take the train from Krakow to Lublin. The small Catholic university had one basic flat in which to accommodate its visiting lecturers. Father Karol usually slept on the floor. Anonymously, he donated the salary he was paid to a hardship fund for students.

Students not only enjoyed his courses but found him approachable outside the lecture hall too. He would hear confessions and offer Mass while he was there at Lublin and before having to catch a train back to Krakow.

In November 1956 the Dominican priest who held the Chair of Ethics at the Catholic Unversity of Lublin was transferred to the Angelicum in Rome. Wojtyla succeeded him as Professor at Lublin, a post he would hold for 22 years until Providence decreed that he would take his teaching beyond the confines of Poland!

The Dignity of the Human Person

Having seen their country so humiliated under the Nazi regime, having seen how that regime could so quickly de-humanise so many, and now living under the yoke of atheistic communism, Professor Wojtyla and his colleagues at the Catholic University of Lublin, were keen to engage Poland's youth, its future parents, teachers, priests and leaders of society, in the most basic theological and philosophical questions. They knew only too well that ideas have consequences.

Thus Father Karol was part of the vanguard that was promoting the dignity of the human person. Ideas have consequences and for them it was essential to defend the dignity of the human person – in the basic human social unit of the family, in the mutual self-giving of marriage, in the individual's relationship with society, the world of work and politics.

As they had done from the beginning, the communists in Poland went all out to promote the idea of the human being as just another cog in the great collective. They did all in their power to undermine true human dignity, downgrading marriage, trying to divorce human love and sexuality from procreation, allowing the previously indefensible killing of unborn children by abortion.

From 1957 until 1959 Father Karol developed and delivered a series of lectures entitled *Love and Responsibility*. He later recalled that it was "born of pastoral necessity" as the pastoral priest and professor understood that young people and young couples of the day not only needed but were entitled to a true and complete and holistic understanding and indeed celebration of their vocation as married couples and dignified human beings.

Love and Responsibility would later be published as a book.

Wanda Poltawska

In that and in other courses of lectures he would prepare, Wojtyla would seek input from his wide circle of friends, academics from other disciplines. One such was the philosopher Andrzej Poltawski. He was married to Wanda, a medical doctor and psychiatrist.

Back in February 1941 when the young Karol was still working at the chemical plant, mourning the death of his father and beginning to reconsider his own path in life, a young Polish woman was arrested by the Gestapo in her home town of Lublin.

The 19 year-old Wanda who used to deliver notes and messages on behalf of the resistance, even as she was being led away from her family home thought to herself, "Huh, all these big men just to arrest one girl!"

After being beaten and interrogated at Gestapo headquarters, she was thrown into an underground cell with prostitutes and other criminals in Lublin Castle. From there she was transported to the infamous Ravensbruck concentration camp outside Berlin. There, with some other girls and women, Wanda became one of the Nazis' 'human guinea-pigs' used to perform senseless medical experiments upon. Wanda, for example, had diseased bacilli injected into her bone marrow - in order to see how her body would 'cope'.

As the war was ending and the Red Army was advancing to liberate Ravensbruck concentration camp, the Nazis fled. Before doing so, they had already given up on trying to dispose of the hundreds of corpses they normally incinerated every day. Instead they piled them all into one great hangar. In that cadaverous mound there was also the skeletal figure of the 22 year-old Wanda. Except, out of all the corpses beside her, under her, lying on top of her, she was NOT dead.

When the Russian soldiers entered that building and discovered its macabre contents, they shouted out to their colleagues not to come in, it was just a pile of corpses. At that moment, from somewhere, the left-for-dead Wanda summoned up some scrap of vitality and energy to raise an arm and make a sound. A soldier spotted her; she was saved.

Even as she had been thrown in with those corpses days before, Wanda had told herself that if she were to survive she would become a doctor and use medicine for the good instead of for evil.

Wanda did qualify as a doctor in 1951 and went on to study psychiatry too. In 1947 she had married Andrzej, who went on to become Professor of Philosophy at Warsaw's Theological Academy. They had four daughters, two of whom became doctors, and two artists.

Wanda chose to study psychiatry as she saw it as being the most humane of all branches of medicine, as the psychiatrist in her view "helps the individual to become a mature person who is aware of his or her humanity".

She went on to work in the psychiatric clinic of Krakow's Medical Academy and in an outpatient advisory centre for problem children at the Jagiellonian University in Krakow.

Some time in the late 1950s while caring for a pregnant unmarried girl, Wanda sought the help of Father Karol Wojtyla. It was the start of a lifelong friendship.

Karol Wojtyla the Cardinal Archbishop of Krakow prior to entering the Papal conclave in August 1978.

❧ A MODERN BISHOP ❧

In August 1958 Father Karol and a circle of friends had left Krakow for the countryside as they were to have a holiday kayaking and hiking in the Polish countryside. The first day they had kayaked 15 miles up the River Lyne in the northeast of the country. The group would leave copies of their schedule with family and friends at home, so that they could be reached in case of urgency, messages sent to local post offices and so on.

The Calling of a Bishop

On 5th August a letter was waiting at one such village post office telling Fr Karol to report immediately to the residence of the Primate, Cardinal Wyszynski, in Warsaw. Karol and a couple of friends hitched a ride on a milk cart to the nearest town. In the railway station toilets Karol changed into his clerical cassock before catching the train to Warsaw.

Cardinal Wyszynski informed the 38 year-old priest that Pope Pius XII had named him a bishop and that he would be an auxiliary bishop to Archbishop Baziak in Krakow. When Karol began to protest to the Cardinal that he was too young to be a bishop, the venerable Primate retorted, "time will take care of that"!

When he left the Cardinal's residence, Karol knocked on the door of an Ursuline convent and asked the sisters if he might pray in their chapel. The sisters showed him the way. After some time, when the unknown priest had not emerged the sisters gingerly looked into the chapel. The priest was prostrate on the floor before the tabernacle. The sisters tiptoed out and closed the door again. When more time passed, they went and suggested that the Reverend Father might like some supper? "No," he told them. "My train doesn't leave until midnight and I have a lot to discuss with Our Lord. I'll just stay here, thank you sisters." And stay there before the Blessed Sacrament he did until it was time to catch his train back to Krakow. There he reported to Archbishop Baziak. If the ageing archbishop expected his new young auxiliary to stick around, he got a surprise when Karol explained that he had to get back to the countryside where he had left his friends, and celebrate Sunday Mass for them. His friends were stunned by the news, but Karol reassured them, "Uncle will still be Uncle"!

On the day he had been summoned to Warsaw, a couple of friends of Karol's had had their first child. Uncle Karol performed the baptism on 31st August before leaving for a meeting of the Polish bishops at Czestochowa. He then made a five-day retreat in preparation for his episcopal ordination.

The ceremony took place on 28th September 1958 in Wawel Cathedral, so closely linked to Karol's own sense of vocation and identity as well as to the national identity.

New Ideas

The new young bishop had wanted a type of liturgical 'commentator' to explain to the congregation what was happening at various points of the rich and symbol-laden consecration service. Archbishop Baziak would not hear of such intrusion into the ancient and venerable liturgy. Wojtyla, instead, got hold of a translation of the rite from Latin into Polish and some friends bound together the mimeographed pages to make little booklets for everyone attending the ceremony.

As auxiliary bishop of the ancient diocese of Krakow, Karol moved out of his residence of the previous six years, the Dean's House that he shared with Father Rozycki at 19 Kanonzica Street, and into the episcopal palace at 3 Franciszkanska Street.

Bishop Wojtyla continued his chaplaincy work in Krakow and his lecturing as Professor of Ethics at the Catholic University of Lublin, even if his visits there became slightly less frequent. Of course as bishop he now had many more pastoral responsibilities and calls on his time: ordaining deacons and subdeacons, administering the

Sacrament of Confirmation, pastoral visits to parishes throughout the archdiocese...

An Open House

Administration may be a burden for those with pastoral responsibility but Bishop Wojtyla saw the episcopal ministry as being primarily one of teaching and preaching and he was in much demand as a preacher of retreats.

When he became diocesan bishop some five years later, the bishop's palace became a type of open house where anyone could come to see the bishop. He later remembered, "the bishop's home was nearly always occupied, full of life. And the Sisters of the Sacred Heart had to feed everybody...!"

Five months after Wojtyla was consecrated bishop, Pope John XXIII, on 25th January 1959, announced the convocation of the Second Vatican Council. In December of that year Bishop Wojtyla submitted an essay on the crisis of humanism to the papal commission set up to prepare the Council.

Nowa Huta

That same month of 1959 the auxiliary bishop of Krakow celebrated midnight Mass not in Wawel cathedral or some other splendid church, but in an open field. The communists were building a new town outside Krakow called Nowa Huta. It was to be a new model town for the new communist man; a town with no room for God. No church would be built there.

Bishop Wojtyla, like all the episcopate, and like the priests and laypeople of Poland, were used to discrimination and harassment towards the Church from the communists. But this, Wojtyla the shepherd, could not take. Expecting people to live and work in a town for the good of the State, yet have nowhere to go to worship Almighty God and have the needs of their own souls catered for! No!

In the coming years the bishop would celebrate midnight Mass in the field at Nowa Huta, not missing the parallels with the Holy Family who on that holy night 2,000 years before had had nowhere else to go.

The 'town with no room for God' became something of a cause celebre among concerned Catholics in other countries. Wojtyla and the parishioners of Nowa Huta began to build the church. The communists would dismantle the work they had done. The parishioners would start again.

Eventually a stalemate seemed to be reached. The communist authorities confronted the bishop who reputedly told them, "I suggest that you allow the people to build their church. Otherwise I shall go out there and join them and who knows what will happen if you try to arrest their bishop..." The church was built.

It was designed to be modern and striking in its architecture. It would represent an ark in which Mary, Queen of Poland would gather and lead her Son's people to safety. Eventually, on 13th October 1967, permission was granted by the civil, communist, authorities. The next day Wojtyla, by then archbishop, led a ground-breaking ceremony and himself swung a pickaxe as he helped dig the first section of the church's foundations.

As the town continued to grow, so did the pastoral needs. A district of the new town had no church. A young priest came to Wojtyla, by then a cardinal, in 1970 and said "We need a church in Miestrzjowice. They might put me in prison, but I'm ready to begin." Wojtyla gave the 33 year-old priest his blessing. Father Jozef Kurzeja bought a plot of land and built a little wooden dwelling, rather like a shed. He erected an altar on the side of it and began to offer Holy Mass there. He was persecuted and harassed by the communist authorities. On Christmas Eve 1971, Bishop Wojtyla once again offered Holy Mass in an open field, this times at Miestrzjowice. Thousands of people attended that Mass and the bishop defended his priest in the face of the persecution he suffered from the communists. But the harassment continued – in the street, at his apartment, at the little wooden chapel, taken in for interrogation. Finally, on the 15th August 1976 Father Jurzeja suffered heart failure and died, aged 39. His fearless and faithful ministry and his early death made an impression on Wojtyla and as Pope in 1983 he consecrated the church built in Miestrzejowice.

Popular Devotion

As well as facing up to the authorities at every turn, Bishop Wojtyla encouraged and supported all the traditional popular devotions of the people and would join them on pilgrimages to local holy places. The communists were determined to stamp out the traditional Corpus Christi procession through Krakow. Wojtyla debated and negotiated with the communist authorities who tried to limit the procession to an extremely short route. Eventually a compromise was reached. Along the route various 'stations' or altar-stops were set up. Wojtyla would preach at each station. Thousands upon thousands of Krakowians would throng the streets for this event which as well as being a devotional affair became a major resistance in the face of the atheistic powers running the country. In 1977, for example, in his sermon at the first station, Wojtyla warned the authorities, "Awareness of human rights keeps growing" and "These rights are undeniable".

In June 1962 Archbishop Baziak died. On 16th July, feast of Our Lady of Mount Carmel, the Metropolitan Chapter elected Bishop Wojtyla as Vicar Capitular, that is he would fulfill the functions of the diocesan archbishop until such time as Rome would appoint someone to the vacant see.

Shortly after, while he was making a pastoral visitation to an outlying parish, Wojtyla heard of a problem back in Krakow. The communists wanted to take over the archdiocesan seminary to use as a teacher training college. This was the building the young Wojtyla and his fellow 'secret seminarians' had patched up after the Gestapo had left it in near ruins in 1945. Hearing that now 17 years later the communists planned to take it, the bishop cut short his pastoral visit and came straight back to Krakow. There he demanded to see the local secretary of the communist party. His actions paid dividends. The party would use the third floor for its college but the seminary would retain the first two floors and thus control of the building.

The Second Vatican Council

The Council was to begin on 11th October, feast of the Motherhood of Mary, 1962. Wojtyla left Krakow for Rome on the 5th October. On a personal level he was preoccupied by the news of one of his dearest friends. Wanda Poltawska had been diagnosed with a cancerous tumour on her neck. Having arrived in Rome for the Council, Wojtyla wrote a letter, in Latin, to the stigmatist Capuchin friar at San Giovanni Rotondo. He asked Padre Pio for prayers for his friend the mother of four young daughters. At the time

Padre Pio was receiving over 2,000 letters a week from all over the world. When the priest who was acting as his secretary read out this letter, Pio said, "Oh, this one we cannot refuse."

A day or two later when Wojtyla telephoned home to Krakow on the evening of the day of Wanda's operation, he was devastated. Andrzej Poltawski told him that they had not operated. Wojtyla feared that that meant it was too late. Instead Andrzej told him that a final pre-operative x-ray showed that the tumour had quite simply disappeared!

Bishop Wojtyla wrote again to Padre Pio, in Latin, thanking him for his prayers and telling him that his friend was now well. On receiving this letter Padre Pio told his priest assistant, "Keep both those letters. Some day they will be important."

Love and Responsibility

In 1960 Wojtyla's book *Love and Responsibility* was published. Within a few years it was being translated and published in other languages. As one writer has summarised it, "Freedom, not prohibition, is the framework of Wojtyla's sexual ethic. We are made as free creatures so that we can dispose of ourselves as a gift to others. We are free so that we can love freely, and thus truly."

When he was made Archbishop of Krakow, Wojtyla set up an Institute for the Family and placed Wanda Poltawska in charge of it. Dr Poltawska obviously had a great input into the marriage preparation programme in the Krakow diocese. She also, at the Archbishop's request, drew up a programme of study for seminarians of the diocese to understand the Church's teaching on marriage and the family. As Pope, John Paul II made Wanda and her husband Andrzej members of the Pontifical Council for the Family which he founded.

During his short reign Pope John XXIII had set up a Papal Commission for the *Study of Problems of the Family, Population and Birth Rate*. His successor Pope Paul VI reappointed the commission to continue its work. As its title suggested, the commission's task was to look at questions of population and birth rate but the world's media focused on the question of artificial and chemical contraception. Pope Paul VI was well aware of Archbishop Wojtyla's *Love and Responsibility* (this had been translated into French, a language Paul VI was proficient in) and appointed him to his Papal Commission. In June 1966 the Commission sent a memorandum, approved by a majority of its members, to the Pope. Broadly speaking, it argued that in certain circumstances the use of artificial contraception would be morally licit. This memorandum was leaked to the press – in order to put more pressure on His Holiness Pope Paul VI - and dubbed 'the Majority Report'.

That very year, 1966, Archbishop Wojtyla had set up his own diocesan commission to study the questions put to the Papal Commission. As archbishop he took an active part in its discussions along with the various experts gathered by his diocesan Institute for the Family.

Humanae Vitae

The communist authorities of Poland had refused Archbishop Wojtyla permission to travel abroad for that fateful meeting of the Papal Commission which produced the so-called 'Majority Report'. Paul VI had to wrestle with all that his commission had produced and decide what, in fact, was the true and lasting teaching of the Church on the questions put.

In February 1968 Archbishop Wojtyla sent Pope Paul VI the outcome of his own diocesan commission on the question. Written in French so that the Pope could read it without any need of translation, the Krakow commission argued for the dignity of man and woman in marriage, the equality of each in the partnership and the co-operation required from both in planning their family. In brief, echoing the philosophy found in *Love and Responsibility*, the Krakow Commission wanted a papal encyclical (which the whole world was waiting for) to take a positive Christian-humanistic approach to marital spirituality and sexuality. Dr Wanda Poltawska, head of Krakow's Institute for the Family recognised that this also required "a great ascetic effort and mastery of self".

Eventually, on 25th July 1968, Pope Paul published his encyclical 'on human life', *Humanae Vitae*. He would suffer greatly from the large-scale rejection of his teaching on the part of so many theologians and intelligentsia in the rich West. Even some bishops dissented from this Papal teaching.

From his mountain-top monastery in southern Italy, the stigmatist Padre Pio penned the last letter he would ever write (he died on 23rd September that year). It was a letter thanking Pope Paul for his clear and beautiful restatement of Christian teaching on the family and human life. Six years previously Padre Pio had answered Archbishop Wojtyla's plea to intercede for the life of one Dr Wanda Poltawska. Pio had said that this was a request that he could not refuse!

A Young Cardinal

The Second Vatican Council took place in 'sessions' when the world's bishops would gather in Rome for the debates then return to their own dioceses while various commissions worked on the deliberations of the Council Fathers. In January 1964 Bishop Wojtyla, who had been running the diocese as Vicar Capitular, was named Archbishop of Krakow by Paul VI and installed as such in

Wawel Cathedral on 8th March. In June 1967 Pope Paul VI made him a cardinal: at only 47 he was the second youngest in the college.

Wojtyla played a full and active role at the Council, making several 'interventions' or speeches. In the first Session, he addressed the Council Fathers on reform of the sacred liturgy and again on revelation. In the autumn 1963 session he spoke on the Church as the People of God, in September 1964 he intervened on the question of religious freedom and in October of that year on the lay vocation.

Drafting *Gaudium et Spes*

That October he also intervened on the 'Church in the modern world' and from January to April the following year, 1965, he took part in a subcommission re-drafting the Council document (*Gaudium et Spes*) on that same topic. Cardinal Wojtyla intervened twice in the final session of Vatican II; on the responsibilities of religious freedom, and on the Christian understanding of 'the world' and the problem of modern atheism.

While listening to debates in the Council chamber that was St Peter's Basilica, Wojtyla also wrote; articles, poems, drafts of pastoral letters. As a university lecturer and professor he had been known to work through his correspondence while listening to a student and then sum up exactly the student's presentation! So, it seems, he could listen attentively to the debates conducted in Latin on the Council floor, and continue with his writing. He would send poems and articles home to Poland for publication in theological journals there, so that he might share some of that experience of the Council with his compatriots immediately.

Most of his writing throughout his life as bishop and pope, though, was done on his knees. Every day he made two or three hours to spend before the Blessed Sacrament where he would write his speeches, conferences, pastoral letters and so on. He once wrote, "Prayer makes the priest and through prayer the priest becomes himself."

During those years of the Council he also made the acquaintance of many of the world's bishops. Writing some forty years later in *Rise, let us be on our way*, Wojtyla remembered a few bishops in particular that had impressed him. He wrote rather touchingly of one priest who was at the Council as his bishop's theological expert: "I particularly remember the then very young Professor Ratzinger. ...He was later named Archbishop of Munich by Pope Paul VI, who also made him a cardinal, and he took part in the conclave that elected me to the Petrine ministry. When Cardinal Franjo Seper died, I asked Cardinal Ratzinger to take his place as Prefect of the Congregation for the Doctrine of the Faith. I thank God for the presence and the assistance of this great man, who is a trusted friend."

As well as meeting so many fellow bishops from around the world, the Council afforded Archbishop Wojtyla the opportunity to take part in a pilgrimage of bishops to the Holy Land at the close of the first Session in December 1963. The Council came to its close on 8th December 1965 and the bishops headed home to their own dioceses and countries.

Implementing Vatican II and Personalism

Archbishop Wojtyla wanted to absorb all that had happened during Vatican II and to explore and share that with his own diocese. To this end he wrote the book *Sources of Renewal* and in 1972 opened a diocesan synod which sought to implement the teachings or fruits of Vatican II into diocesan life. He formally closed that diocesan synod when he visited Poland as pope in 1979.

When *Love and Responsibility* had been published in 1960 a senior priest in Krakow had told Wojtyla, "Now you must write a book on The Person". In light of what he, his fellow Poles and countless other Europeans had witnessed and experienced under Nazism and then Communism, Wojtyla agreed that a fully developed philosophy of the human person was required.

Dealing with the deepest subjects, the text did not make for easy reading. When he asked one of his circle, a priest of Krakow, to read it and comment, the two men went for a hike in the hills. The priest ventured that perhaps the first step would be to translate it – from Wojtyla's lofty language into Polish so that he could understand it!

In a letter to Fr Henri de Lubac, Wojtyla summarised well what he was setting out to do: "I devote my very rare free moments to a work that is close to my heart and devoted to the metaphysical sense and mystery of the PERSON. It seems to me that the debate today is being played out on that level. The evil of our times consists in the first place in a kind of degradation, indeed in a pulverization, of the fundamental uniqueness of each human person. This evil is even much more of the metaphysical order than of the moral order. To this disintegration planned at time by atheistic ideologies, we must oppose, rather than sterile polemics, a kind of 'recapitulation' of the inviolable mystery of the person..."

The work was published as *Person and Act* by the Polish Theological Society in 1969. Further revised editions followed and after Wojtyla's election to the papacy it began to be translated into other languages.

Travels as Bishop

In August and September 1969 Cardinal Wojtyla travelled throughout Canada and the United States of America. He visited expatriate Polish communities there but of course got to know many of the local bishops and Cardinals too. In September and October of that year he participated in the Synod of Bishops held in Rome.

The following year he was back in Rome again to participate in another Synod of Bishops. During that synod Pope Paul VI beatified the Polish Franciscan Maximilian Kolbe who had laid down his life in Auschwitz concentration camp.

Speaking in French at a press conference before the beatification, Cardinal Wojtyla said that Maximilian Kolbe's spirit of forgiveness "broke the infernal cycle of hatred".

In February 1973 Cardinal Wojtyla was on another long-distance trip as he visited Australia to represent the Church in Poland at the Eucharistic Congress being held in the Australian capital.

In April 1974 he went to Litomerice in Czechoslovakia for the funeral of Cardinal Trochta who had spent years in communist prisons. The secret police surrounded the church and the local communist authorities had refused permission for Cardinal Wojtyla and two other visiting foreign prelates to concelebrate the funeral Requiem Mass.

Cardinal Wojtyla thus sat in the pews with the congregation and came forward to receive Holy Communion like a layman. At the end of the funeral rites, though, he defied the communist authorities as he stepped forward and gave a funeral oration over the coffin of the deceased cardinal. As he was travelling on to Rome, later that evening Wojtyla stopped off in Vienna and offered his Holy Mass privately in the chapel of the Nunciature.

In October of that year Cardinal Wojtyla served as relator of the Synod of Bishops on evangelisation. During that month in Rome for the synod, he also made a pilgrimage to the tomb of Padre Pio at San Giovanni Rotondo. En route he visited the Eucharistic miracle at Lanciano. There is preserved the sacred host which sometime in the eighth century turned to human flesh and survives to this day. In the visitors' book the Polish cardinal wrote some words from St Thomas Aquinas's hymn *Adoro Te Devote*; "This faith each day deeper be my holding of, daily make me harder hope and dearer love".

Preaching the Papal Lenten Retreat

In 1976 Pope Paul VI invited the vigorous young Polish cardinal to preach the traditional Lenten retreat to the Curia and the papal household. Wojtyla went to the ski resort of Zakopane for a week in February to begin preparing the 22 talks he would be required to give over the course of the papal retreat. Back home in Krakow he dedicated his writing time in the chapel over four days to further work on his texts. Finally in Rome he spent four days at the Polish College finalising the sermons which he would have to preach in Italian.

The core of his theme was a phrase from Vatican II's *Gaudium et Spes*, "it is only in the mystery of the Word made flesh that the mystery of man truly becomes clear." His sermons exploring further this 'Christian humanism' were later published in Poland by the samizdat review *Znak*.

In July of that year he travelled again, this time to the United States to attend the international Eucharistic Congress being held in Philadelphia. He had been invited to preach on the theme of "The Eucharist and Man's Hunger for Freedom".

In the designs of Providence, this cardinal from behind the Iron Curtain was becoming more and better known in many other countries, and in particular he was now well-known to the College of Cardinals and the world-wide episcopate.

He continued to preach the dignity of man and promote his basic rights or freedoms. At the 1977 Synod of Bishops on religious education he said, "One can understand that a man may search and not find; one can understand that he may deny; but it is not understandable that a man may have imposed on him the dictum 'It is forbidden for you to believe'."

Conflict with Communism

By his actions and his preaching at home and around the world Cardinal Wojtyla did not stop reminding the communist regime that its days were numbered. As he had preached at the Corpus Christi procession, human rights were inalienable and the whole world was becoming ever more aware of that.

For their part the communist authorities did not let up their harassment of Church leaders and prominent Catholics. The Cardinal's residence at 3 Franciszkana Street was heavily bugged. His car was constantly tailed. When they wanted to send a particularly strong message to the cardinal one of his elderly priests would be beaten up by the secret police.

For his part the Shepherd of the Flock in Krakow knew that despite such outward restrictions and harassment, a pastor must continue to live in the "joy of the Lord" and in the confidence that being a child of God brought with it. He knew that he, along with Cardinal Wyszinski of Warsaw, represented to the people the true Polish identity. He understood that it was his duty to guard the people's real freedom, their inner liberty, by protecting their true identity and in a sense giving it back to them. That is, dictatorial regimes could oppress and harass but one must not allow them to steal one's very identity, which is exactly what they wanted.

Pope John Paul II on holiday in the Aoste Valley

❧ THE PAPACY ❧

O n the 6th August, Feast of the Transfiguration of Christ, 1978, Pope Paul VI died at the papal summer palace at Castelgandolfo. At that time Cardinal Wojtyla was on his usual summer holiday of the first fortnight of August. He returned to Krakow on the 8th and left for Rome on 11th August. Between the Pope's funeral and the start of the conclave to elect his successor, Wojtyla had remembered on Vatican Radio the keen interest Paul VI had taken in the battle of Nowa Huta. He recalled how the Pope had personally given him a stone from the tomb of St Peter to be placed in the foundations of the Ark church at Nowa Huta.

Conclave

The conclave elected Cardinal Luciani of Venice on 26th August. He would be known as John Paul the First. On the morning of 29th September 1978 he was found dead in bed after suffering a massive heart attack.

A Second Conclave

On the evening of 28th September Cardinal Wojtyla celebrated Holy Mass in Wawel Cathedral at the altar of the Holy Cross of Blessed Queen Jadwiga. It was the feast of

St Wenceslaus and the 20th anniversary of Wojtyla's consecration as a bishop.

Afterwards he attended a party in the house of friends. They had laid out a big display of photographs celebrating their years of kayaking and skiing trips as the circle of friends. A big banner recalled Wojtyla's words of 20 years before, "Uncle will remain Uncle"! His friends noticed that he seemed somewhat subdued and made a deliberate point of thanking each of them for his or her friendship over the years.

The next morning while he was having breakfast at the Archdiocesan Curia a secretary took the phone call announcing the death of John Paul I. Wojtyla went immediately to the chapel. Two days later, on 1st October, he offered a Requiem Mass in the church in the market square in Krakow.

On 2nd October he attended a meeting of a council of the Polish episcopate in Warsaw. He stayed at the Ursuline convent where 20 years previously he had spent hours in prayer after being named a bishop. This time the sisters noted that he looked very serious. The next morning Wojtyla left Warsaw for Rome with Cardinal Wyszinski.

They stayed in the Polish College. They would be locked into the secret conclave in the Vatican on the 14th October. On the 13th Wojtyla received devastating news. One of his closest friends had suffered a massive stroke.

Bishop Andrzej Deskur had been in seminary with him and for some years had been serving the Church in Rome, currently as head of the Pontifical Council for Social Communications. Wojtyla rushed straight to see his old friend at the Gemelli hospital. The next morning he offered his Mass at the Polish College for Bishop Deskur. In the afternoon he went back to the hospital to visit his friend, who was paralysed and barely able to speak. From his bedside, Wojtyla went straight to the Vatican to join his fellow Cardinals processing into the Sistine Chapel to begin the conclave to elect a pope.

Papabile

Cardinal Wojtyla had received a handful of votes in the conclave that elected John Paul I but it had never seemed likely that after 450 years a non-Italian would be considered seriously for the papacy. Cardinal Ratzinger later commented that at the second conclave of 1978, he and other cardinals "felt somewhat depressed. The fact that Providence had said 'no' to our choice was really a very hard blow. However, Luciani's election was not an error. Those 33 days of pontificate have had a role in the history of the Church... His unexpected death also opened the doors to an unexpected choice: that of a Pope who was not Italian."

Cardinal Konig of Austria who had pushed for a non-Italian at the first conclave of 1978 saw Cardinal Wojtyla as the best choice and proposed his idea to Cardinal Wyszinski who thought he was too young. However when the conclave began and an impasse was reached between two Italian candidates, the door opened to Cardinal Wojtyla's supporters. As Wyszinski saw that his protégé seemed more and more likely to accede to the See of Peter he advised him that if he were elected he should accept.

His intellectual clout and involvement in Vatican II had brought him to the attention of many in the college, but it was his pastoral experience, leading a large diocese under difficult circumstances in Communist Poland, that made him an attractive choice. Evidently the Cardinals very quickly came to the conclusion that these qualities were ideal for the Chief Shepherd, Christ's Vicar on Earth, the one who would unite and govern the worldwide Roman Catholic Church.

On the third day of the conclave Karol Wojtyla received the necessary majority of votes to be elected. When the cardinal chamberlain, Jean Villot, approached him to ask if he accepted election to the Petrine Ministry, Wojtyla said: "In the obedience of faith before Christ my Lord, abandoning myself to the Mother of Christ and the Church, and conscious of the great difficulties, I accept." Out of respect for the two popes of the council he took the name John Paul II.

Habemus Papam

An hour later white smoke rose from the chimney of the Sistine Chapel. Immediately, John Paul II broke with the custom that the new Pope should only speak the *urbi et orbi* blessing from the balcony of St Peter's. He made a short speech saying that the cardinals had called him from a far away country, but which was close to Rome through its faith and Christian tradition. He later explained that he was not speaking of geographical distance but of the iron curtain which separated his Poland from the rest of the world that was free to be Christian. The mainly-Italian crowd gathered in the square below had no idea who this Polish pope was. Addressing them in "our Italian language" the man "from a faraway country" soon won them over.

An Historic Papacy

His would be the third-longest papacy in history. For over a quarter of a century Papa Wojtyla would preach and teach on the world stage. From the start, though, it was his personal charisma that won through. As he preached a message the world often did not want to hear, people - especially young people - understood that this was a man who was truly a disciple of the Master he proclaimed. The Pope was obviously a pastor who actually believed and lived what he preached. A whole generation of young Catholics grew up only ever having known one pope, John

Paul II. They have became known as the *John Paul II Generation*.

From that first appearance as pope on the balcony of St Peter's Papa Wojtyla both consoled and challenged the world with his message; *Do not be afraid. Open wide your doors to Christ*. His message was aimed at individual human hearts and also at entire political systems and regimes!

When the world's media announced in October 1978 that a Polish cardinal had been elected pope, the most famous dissident of Soviet Russia, Aleksandr Solzhenitsyn, was living with his family in exile in Vermont, USA. His secretary, the Russian exile Irina Ilovayiska Alberti later told this writer that when he heard the news on the BBC World Service Solzhenitsyn went crazy. "He was jumping up and down and whooping, behaving like we had never seen him before," she remembered. "This changes everything. A Polish pope. It changes everything," she remembered Solzhenitsyn repeating over and over.

Travels

As Bishop of Rome, he continued his tradition of parish visits just as he had done as Archbishop of Krakow. And, of course, he travelled the world, clocking up over 700,000 miles and visiting over 120 countries. He admitted in his memoirs that he enjoyed travel. He also believed that it was part of his ministry as successor to St Peter and Bishop of Rome to journey to visit other local churches, so as to teach and "strengthen the brethren", in particular within those countries that were experiencing difficulties.

On many occasions John Paul travelled to give people back their own identity. In his first return visits to his homeland for a start. As the regime imposed a media blackout, it seemed almost the entire population turned out onto the streets to gather around the Vicar of Christ, who happened to be Polish! The people understood that they did not need the State's newspapers or televisions to tell them who they were. They knew. They were Polish. They were Catholics. They would live in the freedom of the Children of God.

Nicaragua

Karol Wojtyla's experience of living under the communist regime in Poland prepared him well for encountering other dictatorial or 'revolutionary' regimes as pope. In March 1983 at a Papal Mass in Nicaragua, the regime had filled the front sections of the park with Sandinista supporters. Loyal Catholics who had come to hear and listen to the Holy Father were corralled into pens right at the back of the venue. A platform was erected right next to the Papal altar and filled with senior Sandinista members and members of the government. During the Holy Mass they waved their clenched fists and shouted "People's Power". When the time came for the Vicar of Christ to preach his sermon, he could see that the people herded to the rear of the park could hear him because they would applaud and cheer at certain points. When, however, the Pope began to explain how you could not have a 'People's Church' opposed to the legitimate Church, engineers turned down the volume on the Pope's microphone. Other microphones had been secreted among the Sandinista supporters taking up the front section of the park. On cue, these people began to shout and jeer the Holy Father so that he was totally drowned out. The government and party members on their own special podium continued to misbehave with their antics too. Eventually John Paul II summoned up all his full voice and shouted over the mob for silence!

At the end of the Mass the regime arranged for their Sandinista anthem to be played as a recessional hymn as the Pope left the podium. John Paul refused to leave. Instead he stood there, held his papal crozier, the cruciform staff, high over his head and waved it back and forth. The hundreds of thousands of Nicaraguans who had come to see and hear the Holy Father understood. He was there for *them*, as *their* pastor. They roared their approval and even the party-organised hecklers could not drown out their applause. As the event had been televised throughout several Latin-American countries, the regime's attempts to desecrate the Papal Mass backfired on them. When the Pope returned that night to Costa Rica, the people filled the streets, bigger and more enthusiastic crowds than had greeted him the day before. People had begun to see through the Sandinista myth.

Chile

Another papal visit which the local oppressive regime tried to undermine was the Pope's trip to Chile in April 1987. The Holy Father was to beatify a Chilean religious sister during a Mass held in a park in Santiago. The senior cleric in charge of liturgical services during the Pope's visit sensed something was wrong before His Holiness even arrived at the park. The crowds occupying the front sections were not responding as normal Catholics usually did in the preparation for the Pope's arrival.

As the Liturgy of the Word began and the Biblical readings were being proclaimed, a riot started in the section of the crowd to the Pope's left. Then they began to burn tyres that they had brought into the park for the purpose. The Pope and the congregation found it difficult to breathe. Eventually, riot police came in and quelled the disturbance. The local bishops were convinced that the disturbances could not have happened without the connivance of the regime. At the end of Mass, the Holy Father did not move to leave the platform. Instead he knelt down and gazed out at the crowds. The message was clear; *no-one* was going to drive him away. He had come for *them*, the people. The regime and its troublemakers would not make him abandon his flock.

As he was driven back to the nunciature after the Mass, the streets of Santiago were packed as people came out to express their solidarity with the Pope who had refused to give in, who had instead remained in unity with the ordinary faithful.

Writing and Teaching

As Pope, Karol Wojtyla, pastor and professor, issued an unprecedented volume of teaching, using every medium available to a pope plus some new ones. He wrote 14 encyclicals and 36 Apostolic constitutions, letters or exhortations. Uniquely, for a Pope, he also published four books, the first of which sold over 20 million copies (*Crossing the Threshold of Hope, Gift and Mystery, Arise Let us Go* and *Memory and Identity*) as well as a volume of poetry (*Roman Triptych*).

Many of John Paul's teaching documents have rightly come to be seen as classic texts. In particular his great programmatic first encyclical: *Redemptor Hominis*, Mankind's Redeemer. In it Pope John Paul proclaimed to the world that only in Jesus can mankind find true fulfillment, like Saint Augustine, our hearts will be forever restless until they rest in Him.

He later published an encyclical on the Father of mercies in *Dives in Misericordia* and on the Holy Spirit, the Lord and Giver of Life, in *Dominum et Vivificantem*. He wrote and taught of Our Lady, Mother of the Redeemer in *Redemptoris Mater* and of St Joseph, Patron and Protector of the Church in the Apostolic Exhortation *Redemptoris Custos*.

John Paul II also used his weekly meeting with the Faithful and other visitors to Rome to deliver whole series of catechesis as he expounded his teaching on the family, on the human person, and on faith. From 1979 to 1983 in 129 Wednesday audiences John Paul broke new ground in what has become known as the 'Theology of the Body'. Many have argued that his writings on this subject will prove to be one of his most enduring and important contributions to the Church and the World.

The Assasination Attempt

On Wednesday 13th May 1983, the weekly Papal audience, to be held outside in St Peter's Square, was scheduled for 5pm to avoid the pilgrims having to be outside in the worst of the summer heat.

The Pope was being driven in an open vehicle through the crowds to allow as many as possible to be near the Vicar of Christ before he arrived at his throne set up on the steps of St Peter's. As was his habit, John Paul had accepted a little child into his arms and after kissing her, handed her back to her parents.

At that moment a shot rang out. Then another. And another. The Pope fell into the arms of his secretary Monsignor Stanislaw Dziwisz. He was bleeding profusely. Quickly transferred to an ambulance, he was sped to Rome's Gemelli polyclinic. The journey that should have taken 20 minutes was accomplished in eight.

The bullet had passed through the Pope's body, wounding him in the stomach, the right elbow and the left index finger. The bullet then fell onto the floor of the vehicle between the Holy Father and Msgr Dziwisz.

The attacker had been a professional assassin, the Turk Ali Agca. As the Pope's secretary later remarked, "Agca shot to kill. That shot should have been fatal."

The other two shots fired by Agca wounded two pilgrims who were standing near to where the 'popemobile' was passing at that moment.

As the ambulance sped to the hospital, before losing consciousness, John Paul told his secretary that he forgave his attacker.

When he came to the following afternoon, the Pope asked Msgr Dziwisz if they had yet said Vespers. His secretary had to tell him gently that it was now the next day!

Pope John Paul II talks with his would-be assassin Mehmet Ali Agca during a private meeting in Agca's prison cell in 1983.

Having lost so much blood the Holy Father very nearly died and the doctors had suggested to his secretary that he administer the 'last rites' which he did immediately.

The medics gave the Pope a blood transfusion. His body rejected that blood. Then some doctors in the hospital gave their own blood and this second transfusion went well. They could then operate to work on his severely damaged colon. In the circumstances, they understandably ignored the relatively minor injury of the broken finger. In the end, that healed by itself.

At the beginning of June the Pope left the hospital and returned to his apartment in the Apostolic palace at the Vatican.

John Paul's recovery was set back when he began to suffer terrible fever and weaken again. It turned out that he had been affected by a cytomegalovirus through that first blood transfusion. He had to return to hospital and after intensive treatment was strong enough to undergo further surgery to complete the operation carried out on the day of the attack.

On 13th August, he was discharged from hospital. In October, five months after the attempt on his life, he was back in St Peter's Square to receive the Faithful once more. His faithful secretary noted that the Pope, "showed not a trace of fear, nor even of stress, although the doctors had warned that this was a possibility."

Instead John Paul II told the crowds who had gathered to see him, "Could I forget that the event in St Peter's Square took place on the day and at the hour when the first appearance of the Mother of Christ to the poor little peasants has been commemorated for over sixty years at Fatima in Portugal? For, in everything that happened to me on that very day, I felt that extraordinary motherly protection and care, which turned out to be stronger than the deadly bullet."

Forgiving his Attacker

During the Christmas season the Holy Father visited Ali Agca in his Roman jail.

He later reported that he had spoken "at length" with his attacker. The Pope well understood that Agca was a professional assassin; that is that the attack was not his own initiative, but that someone else had commissioned him to kill the Pope.

Referring to the attempt on his life, John Paul said in *Memory & Identity*, "I think it was one of the final convulsions of the arrogant ideologies unleashed during the twentieth century. Both Fascism and Nazism eliminated people. So did Communism."

One year to the day after the attempt to 'eliminate' him, the Vicar of Christ made a pilgrimage to the Marian shrine at Fatima. The bullet that had passed through his body without killing him was placed into the crown that adorned the statue of Our Lady of Fatima.

John Paul the Priest

As the Church celebrated the 50th anniversary of his ordination to the priesthood John Paul wrote that the priest "must always be a *man of knowledge* in the highest and most religious sense of the term. He must possess and pass on that 'knowledge of God' which is not a mere deposit of doctrinal truths but a personal and living experience of the

Mystery, in the sense spoken of by the Gospel of Saint John in the great priestly prayer: 'This is eternal life, that they *know* you, the only true God, and Jesus Christ whom you have sent" (*John* 17:3).

In that reflection on his priestly vocation and ministry (*Gift and Mystery*) John Paul quoted from a prayer that he himself prayed, in Latin, every day. He also had it reproduced in both Latin and English at the end of the book. In the Litany of Our Lord Jesus Christ, Priest and Victim, he prayed among other things, "That you may kindly provide your people with pastors after your own heart, hear us, we beseech you" and "That through them you may kindly promote the veneration of the Blessed Sacrament all over the world, hear us, we beseech you".

In the Footsteps of the Saints

Our Lord gave to St Peter the keys of the Kingdom of Heaven. As Peter's successor, John Paul II canonised more saints than any of his predecessors. He truly believed in the communion of saints and knew that the prayers of the saints in Heaven, the Church Triumphant, could benefit us here on earth in the Church Militant. On a piece of white card he had a litany of Polish saints that he prayed to every day, wherever he was in the world. As he 'made' new ones he added them in pen to his list! This man, as priest, as bishop, as pope, truly felt a strong link with the saints of his native land who had lived the Gospel before him. Every time he entered his cathedral in Krakow he felt awed to be in the presence of Polish saints buried or venerated there.

And he had every confidence in Divine Providence. If God had called a Polish bishop to be Supreme Pontiff, Christ's Vicar on earth, then it was for a reason. Karol Wojtyla would bring with him all that he had learned as a layman, as a priest and as a bishop in Poland to his task of leading the Universal Church.

This quiet confidence in who he was and what he was called to be, helped explain the strength that seemed to flow from him, that people always felt when they were in his presence.

And that confidence and strength came too from his own total dependency on the Divine Mercy. His hours spent in prayer every day of his life. His motto ever since he had been consecrated a bishop, *Totus Tuus*, Completely Yours, drawn from St Louis de Montfort's Consecration to the Blessed Virgin Mary which Wojtyla discovered on the night-shift at the quarry.

Major reform, consolidation and renewal

As pope, John Paul reformed the Roman Curia, the Vicar of Christ's institutional means of governing the worldwide Church and protecting the deposit of the Faith.

His papacy saw the reform of the *Code of Canon Law*, in both the Latin-rite and eastern-rite parts of the Church. He continued and developed the system of the Synods of Bishops renewed under Paul VI. In response to one such synod's demands, his papacy saw the mammoth task of producing a universal *Catechism of the Catholic Church*. It fell to his successor to inaugurate the long-awaited concise form of that catechism (in June 2005).

As he had done as Archbishop of Krakow, he encouraged new groups and movements which would help lay people (and indeed priests and religious) to live out their Faith better. In *Rise, let us be on our way* he wrote that "during the years of my ministry in Krakow, I always felt spiritually close to the Focolare movement. ...Since I was called to the See of Peter, I have often received Chiara Lubich, together with representatives of the various branches of the Focolare movement."

In that text he also highlighted the Italian-born Communione e Liberazione movement, the Neocatechumenal Way and Jean Vanier's L'Arche and Foi et Lumiere. When he gathered all the new ecclesial movements around him in St Peter's Square in May 1988, he described it as being like a new Pentecost.

Apart from Chiara Lubich, another modern-day foundress that John Paul got to know as soon as possible was Mother Teresa of Calcutta. Everyone who saw them together could see that there was a real spark of friendship and mutual esteem between them, a sense of recognition of the Holy Spirit at work in the other.

In *Rise, let us be on our way*, John Paul wrote, "In the days immediately following my election to the See of Peter, I met this great little missionary sister, who from then on would often visit me to tell me where and when she had succeeded in opening new houses to provide a home for the poorest."

In fact, as Pope he told Mother Teresa to come to see him whenever she was in Rome. Thus, when after Mother Teresa had opened her first house in Scotland and addressed a rally in support of the pro-life cause, the crowds gathered in the courtyard outside the papal palace at Castelgandolfo a few days later had a surprise. After addressing the assembled throng, the Pope beckoned over to a stooped little figure behind the window to come and join him on the balcony. He then proceeded to share with the crowds how Mother Teresa had told him about the beautiful gathering she had attended in Glasgow in support of the unborn baby. It was he who had told Mother Teresa, in the earliest days of his pontificate, to 'go public' in defending the unborn baby. Soon Mother Teresa was invited to speak and witness world-wide in defence of life and spoke up for the unborn child when she received her Nobel Peace Prize in 1979.

When he made a papal visit to India, John Paul visited Mother Teresa's Home for the Dying, known in Hindi as Immaculate Heart House.

In the same book, *Rise...*, he wrote, "I thank God that I was privileged to beatify her on 19th October 2003, around the time of the 25th anniversary of my pontificate."

Points of controversy

John Paul II did all he could to promote inter-religious dialogue and throughout his pontificate, he intuitively offered significant gestures which could be difficult to follow up practically and theologically.

In an age of powerful images, few could forget his gathering of religious leaders at Assisi. For some Catholics, though, it was a hard act to accept. They argued that to see the Vicar of Christ surrounded by leaders of so many man-made religions made it seem as if he were just one among many religious leaders.

John Paul II presided over a general improvement in the Church's dealing with the Jewish religion. He was the first Pope to visit the synagogue of Rome, and coined a famous phrase when he embraced the world's Jews as "our elder brothers."

In his dealings with Islam, many Catholics were left scandalised and confused when he kissed a copy of the Koran in May 1999 and when, at the Ommayadi Mosque in Syria in 2001, he prayed that St John the Baptist would protect Islam! He may have meant to pray for protection for individual Muslims but as Pope, they said, he could not pray for the protection of a man-made religion.

It was a great regret to John Paul II that the clerical child abuse scandals continued in America and elsewhere throughout his papacy. Despite one or two attempts at the beginning of his pontificate to defend orthodox Catholic doctrine, those promoting dissent from Catholic teaching seemed to grow stronger and bolder as his pontificate proceeded and then drew to a close. Bishops in certain countries, sometimes even those raised to the cardinalate, felt themselves at liberty to undermine papal and apostolic teaching with impunity.

John Paul himself admitted that he had been a poor disciplinarian during his pontificate. In *Rise...* he wrote "The pastor's role also includes admonishing. I think that, in this category, I have perhaps done too little."

Yet despite his perceived shortcomings as 'governor' of the Church or his perceived failure to stamp out the heresy of Modernism from seminaries and Church institutions, people recognised and loved the human qualities of the man. Anyone who met him was impressed by his presence, his obvious prayerfulness and his regard and concern for each individual that he met. (After all, 'personalism' was central to his philosophy of Christian humanism.)

Defending Life to the End

From his days as a country curate in the Polish countryside, as a student chaplain and university lecturer and professor, from his time as an auxiliary bishop, then Archbishop and Cardinal and as Vicar of Christ, John Paul II promoted the dignity of man. He had seen the horrors of war at first hand and had lived under two totalitarian regimes. Like Wanda Poltawska and so many of his friends and compatriots, he had seen how quickly men and women could become de-humanised and caught up in a system perpetrating evil.

Throughout his pontificate he consistently defended human life from its earliest moments until its natural end and explained Catholic teaching as to why. Without fear or favour he faced up to governments to defend the weakest and the tiniest. His own dying - in the very week that an American court would authorise the starvation of a handicapped woman Terri Schiavo – was a testimony to the dignity of old age and natural death.

When his health deteriorated in his final years, John Paul II refused to be hidden away. The whole world witnessed his heroic battle to continue life as normally as possible as his body succumbed to Parkinson's disease. Various treatments and drug regimens sometimes seemed to give a temporary relief and then the suffering would again be evident as the Supreme Pontiff struggled to read a sermon.

As the ravages of that cruel disease became ever more apparent there were those in the world who thought it would be more dignified for him to have remained out of sight. For others, it was a clear message of the important place that the elderly, the infirm, the disabled *should* have in our lives and in our society.

For his part, John Paul II, the Polish pastor who never missed an occasion to teach and witness to the Gospel, saw his own sufferings as part of his overall witness to the world. His key message had long been the importance and uniqueness, the infinite value of each and every individual created by God.

In the very last page of his personal memoir, *Memory & Identity*, the Pope had written, "Yet the passion of Christ on the Cross gave a radically new meaning to suffering, transforming it from within. It introduced into human history, which is the history of sin, a blameless suffering, accepted purely for love." His final word on the theme was, "In the love that pours forth from the heart of Christ, we find hope for the future of the world. Christ has redeemed the world: 'By his wounds we are healed'. (*Isaiah* 53:5)"

John Paul's Warnings for the Future

In that book that his publishers had called "an intellectual and spiritual testament", published shortly before he died, John Paul testified to the great themes that had formed his outlook, his life, his pontificate. He was at great pains to issue a very particular warning to Europe:

"Let us now consider a question of great importance for the history of Europe in the twentieth century. It was a regularly elected parliament that consented to Hitler's rise to power in Germany in the 1930s. And the same *Reichstag*, by delegating full powers to Hitler (*Ermachtagunsgesetz*) paved the way for his policy of invading Europe, for the establishment of concentration camps, and for the implementation of the so-called 'final solution' to the Jewish question, that is to say to the elimination of millions of the sons and daughters of Israel. Suffice it to recall these events, so close to us in time, in order to see clearly that law established by man has definite limits, which it must not overstep. They are the limits established by the law of nature, through which God himself safeguards man's fundamental good. Hitler's crimes had their Nuremberg, where those responsible were judged and punished by human justice. In many cases, however, this element is lacking, even if there always remains the supreme judgement of the Divine Legislator. A profound mystery surrounds the manner in which Justice and Mercy meet in God when he judges men and their history."

And once again, John Paul II, tireless defender of human rights – which are fundamentally linked to respecting the laws of God and of nature – reminded legislators one last time that they were overstepping the mark. He said, "From this perspective, as we enter a new century and a new millennium, we must question certain legislative choices made by the parliaments of today's democratic regimes. The most immediate example concerns abortion laws. When a parliament authorises the termination of pregnancy, agreeing to the elimination of the unborn child, it commits a grave abuse against an innocent human being, utterly unable to defend itself. Parliaments which approve and promulgate such laws must be aware that they are exceeding their proper competence and placing themselves in open conflict with God's law and the law of nature."

From his earliest years, the Blessed Mother of God had been Karol Wojtyla's guide and consolation. As he sought to promote the cause of life in face of the pervasive 'culture of death' throughout his papacy, he knew, as he wrote in *Evangelium Vitae*, that "Mary thus helps the Church to *realise that life is always at the centre of a great struggle* between good and evil, between light and darkness."

❧ JOHN PAUL'S LEGACY ❧

Few were very surprised when it was announced that Pope Benedict XVI would beatify John Paul II only six years after his death. While since his own election Pope Benedict had resorted to the earlier custom of candidates being beatified by the Local Ordinary, he made an exception to his self-imposed rule when he travelled to England in 2010 to beatify Cardinal John Henry Newman. No-one doubted that he would not also delight in beatifying his dear friend John Paul II.

Their mutual esteem is forever recorded in the then-Cardinal Ratzinger's address at John Paul's funeral when he imagined the late Pontiff as "standing at the window of the Father's house". And in the biographical memoir *'Rise, Let Us Be On Our Way'* published the year before his death, John Paul stated of Ratzinger, "I thank God for the presence and assistance of this great man, who is a trusted friend."

How to understand this great speed of John Paul II's Beatification? What is clear is that it is not John Paul's papacy that is being beatified, but the man himself, Karol Wojtyla who became Pope John Paul II.

Everyone realises that there were aspects of John Paul's papacy which could have been better. His handling -or not- of clerical child abuse scandals, the scandal of Marcel

Maciel, founder of the Legionaries of Christ, the failure to bring back into the fold the estranged Lefevbrists, the perception of a nod to synchretism with the Assisi gatherings of various religions, John-Paul's kissing of the Muslim Koran, the poor quality of episcopal appointments in many countries, the degrading and often scandalous Papal liturgies on John Paul's travels when the Vicar of Christ was incensed by shamans or 'exorcised' by bare-breasted pagan priestesses.

What everyone also realises is that Papa Wojtyla was a "giant of a man"; a man of deep spirituality and profound charity. He truly strived his utmost to love God and neighbour. And in the second half of the twentieth century, a time of growing utilitarianism and increasingly aggressive secularism, humanism, atheism, everyone -friend or foe- recognises that John Paul II was a great defender of the dignity of the human person; defender of the inalienable right to life, defender of the family, promoter of the Culture of Life.

He was fearless in his attempts to call the world to Reason, a work continued equally fearlessly by his successor, who prayed at his own inauguration that he would "not flee from the wolves". John Paul's outreach to the young was successful because they recognised that he genuinely did love them, that he was a genuine man of God and true pastor.

Polish priest Dr Slawomir Oder was the Postulator of John Paul's Cause for Beatification. He caused a stir when in 2010 he published a book and revealed that John Paul, even as Pope, continued his practices of bodily mortification, such as self-flagellation. As priest and then bishop he often slept on the floor as an act of mortification. The revelation of these practices was deemed 'indelicate' by some. However, anyone who knew much about John Paul's life would find such practices completely normal. As we have pointed out, from a young age he was a member of the Third Order of Carmel. It was the Carmelites' tradition to scourge themselves three times during the week, while reciting Psalm 50, the Miserere. (Indeed, in his 'personal reflections', *Memory and Identity,* he expounds on the Miserere, calling it "one of the most beautiful prayers that the Church inherited from the Old Testament".) Apparently, as a bishop and as Pope, John Paul would particularly perform such self-mortification and penance before ordaining men to the priesthood or episcopate.

What was evident to all was his total devotion to the *Theotokos*, the Mother of God and, as proclaimed by Vatican II, Mother of the Church. His personal motto of '*Totus Tuus*', 'completely yours', showed his complete devotion to the service of the Lord through the intercession of Mary.

Fr Slawomir identified that John Paul's manner of living his various infirmities, particularly his final illness and his approach to death, was also a great witness to the Church and the world. Few could forget his final appearance at the window of his apartment overlooking St Peter's Square. Ravaged by the final stages of Parkinson's disease, he ignored any thought of self or image or ego, in order to give his paternal blessing one final time to the assembled crowds -and *urbe et orbi*- that Easter Sunday, 2005.

John Paul's Will and Testament, first written in 1979 and modified and updated every year during the retreat of the Pontifical Household, is also evidence provided by Fr Slawomir of the Pope's complete and utter commitment and abandonment to God. During the spiritual exercises of 1980 (24th February to 1st March) he wrote:

"Once again I wish to entrust myself totally to the Lord's grace. He will decide when and how I am to end my earthly life and my pastoral ministry. In life as in death, *Totus Tuus*, through the Immaculate. By already accepting this death, I hope that Christ give me the grace for this last passage, that is (my) Pasch. I equally hope that he renders it useful for this more important cause I try to serve: the salvation of human beings, the protection of the human family, in all nations and among all peoples (among these I am thinking in particular of my own earthly country), useful for those who, in a special way, have been entrusted to me, in the Church, for the glory of the same God."

On 5th March 1982 he added: "The attempt on my life, on 13th May 1981, has confirmed, in a certain sense, the accuracy of the words written during the 1980 spiritual exercises (24th February -1st March). I feel even more deeply that I am completely in the Hands of God - and I remain constantly available to my Lord, entrusting myself to Him in His Immaculate Mother (*Totus Tuus*)."

It has often been reported that John Paul said that the happiest day of his life was when in 2000 he canonised St Faustina Kowalska and declared the Feast of the Divine Mercy, as asked for in the apparitions of the Lord to her.

Indeed, in *Memory and Identity*, *Personal Reflections*, his final personal memoir, published in 2005, John Paul wrote, "The patrimony of (Sr Faustina's) spirituality was of great importance, as we know from experience, for the resistance against the evil and inhuman systems of the time. The lesson to be drawn from all this is important not only for the Poles, but also in every part of the world where the Church is present. This became clear during the beatification and canonisation of Sister Faustina. It was as if Christ had wanted to say through her: 'Evil does not have the last word!'"

Listing the highlights of John Paul's legacy, the Postulator of his Cause, Fr Slawomir Oder, concluded with his entrusting of the world to the Divine Mercy. Fr Slawomir recalled, "In August 2002, in Lagiewniki, where Sr Faustina lived and died, John Paul II entrusted the world to the Divine Mercy, to the unlimited trust in God the merciful, to the One who has been a source of inspiration, but also of strength, for his service as Successor of Peter."

The Polish pope, who instituted the feast of Divine Mercy, the man of God who on that same Feast nine years later would become Blessed John Paul II, said at Lagiewniki on 17th August 2002: "So today, in this Sanctuary, I solemnly wish to entrust the world to Divine Mercy. I do so with the burning desire that the message of God's merciful love, proclaimed through Saint Faustina, may reach all the inhabitants of the earth and fill their hearts with hope. May this message spread from this place to our beloved homeland and throughout the world. May the binding promise of the Lord Jesus be fulfilled: from here must come forth 'the spark that will prepare the world for his final coming'."